PRAISE FOR BUSINESS IN BLUE JEANS

"This is the best little "how-to" book for starting and running a small business I've come across. Don't even think about going into business without it. And if you are already in business, this book is a must-read."

LARRY WINGET
Television personality and five-time bestselling author, including
the #1 bestseller: *Shut Up, Stop Whining and Get A Life*

"Everything you need to start your own business is here! Susan delivers much more than the usual "how-to" stuff, instead guiding you to first build the mindset to achieve your dreams. How I wish I had *Business in Blue Jeans* when I started my own business ten years ago!"

DAVID MEERMAN SCOTT
Bestselling author of *The New Rules of Marketing and PR*,
now in over 25 languages from Bulgarian to Vietnamese

"*Business in Blue Jeans* is a strong book of advice for people seeking to find their own way to do business. It's filled with bravery and a lot of opportunities to bring yourself up to a new level. Susan Baroncini-Moe has your homework right here. Get on it."

CHRIS BROGAN
CEO and President of Human Business Works,
Co-author of *The Impact Equation*

"Susan shows you how to have a business and a life; what an amazingly refreshing concept."

JOHN JANTSCH
Author of *Duct Tape Marketing* and
The Commitment Engine

"*Business in Blue Jeans* is a rich framework that will help you create and grow a successful business on your terms. A wonderful combination of actionable advice and insights, it will change how you think and how you approach business."

JOHN MICHAEL MORGAN
Author of *Brand Against the Machine*

"In *Business in Blue Jeans,* Susan delivers an entire college education on entrepreneurship. You'll have homework, but you won't have to sit through classes and boring lectures."

BRIAN HALLIGAN
HUBSPOT CEO

"Some people think that if you want to create a business around your life, it is because you're lazy and want to get rich quick. What the masters know is that creating a business around your life actually takes a lot of hard work and dedication.

Business in Blue Jeans helps you define this path and creates a roadmap for the journey. Sure, you get to wear blue jeans, but you're going to get them all worn in by putting your passion into a business that matters. *Business in Blue Jeans* is both a practical and powerful read for those looking to create the life they were meant to lead."

MITCH JOEL
President of Twist Image
Author, Blogger, Podcaster, *Six Pixels of Separation*

"*Business in Blue Jeans* is real, relevant, and revolutionary. Real, because Susan has an amazing ability to get right to the core of the matter; relevant, because it's full of real-world examples and practical tips that are immediately applicable to any business; and revolutionary, because I guarantee it will permanently change your approach to running and growing a successful business."

BEN COPE
Internet Genius and Web Developer

"New and existing businesses—you need this book. A thorough, complete how-to guide, this should serve as *the* textbook for branding. Perfectly penned; Baroncini-Moe aced this."

CHRIS REIMER
Author of the upcoming book, *The Impossible Contract*

"Susan Baroncini-Moe was made to write this book. She was made to help others to take their business to new levels, but do that in a way that's true to themselves."

There are way too many people who spend their lives building businesses that aren't true to who they are. So they wind up having a "business mid-life crisis" because as their business grows, they like it less and less.

Susan will help you to build a business around your own strengths, talents, and passions, so as it grows you'll love it more and more. In fact, Susan Baroncini-Moe will help you to grow a business that will fit like your favorite pair of blue jeans."

MITCH MATTHEWS
Co-founder, The BIG Dream Gathering
mitchmatthews.com

"I thought I knew the basics of being a small business owner and I needed some advanced tactics to grow my business. Wow! I thought wrong! Susan Baroncini-Moe's *Business in Blue Jeans* takes the basics of small business and takes them to a whole new level, with insights to take *my* business to a whole new level. Jam-packed with proven usable insights, this book will fast become a staple of small business owners everywhere!"

PHIL GERBYSHAK
Chief Connections Officer, Milwaukee Social Media
Author of 4 books and more than 2,500 articles
focused on small business tips and tricks

"Having worked with Susan, I can tell you that *Business in Blue Jeans* is just like sitting down in person with Susan and her wealth of knowledge. Her words will encourage you, teach you, lead you, and even make you laugh out loud. I felt bigger and bolder and ready to tackle my business with new zeal by the time I was only a few pages in. Whether you're thinking about starting a business or are already well down the path of CEO-dom, you will benefit from reading and applying the lessons in this book."

STEPHANIE HINDERER
CEO, Red Letter Paper Company

"Business in Blue Jeans is a great book both for newbies and those who are established. Susan delivers no-nonsense advice and humor in a very conversational tone like she's talking to a friend."

MIKE STENGER
Social Media Specialist

With expert guidance from Susan Baroncini-Moe and her thought-provoking exercises, I moved through a lot of "brain junk" like self-doubt, fear of failure, and self judgment. I was able to finally begin paying attention to my own voice and discover my true ideas about the kind of career and lifestyle I want.

Best of all, with Susan's help, I'm on a path to create a viable business doing what I love, and I've never been more excited about my future! If you've ever wanted to do more, be more, or create more, *Business in Blue Jeans* will help you do it."

BRANDE PLOTNICK
Tomato Envy

"As a business owner and coach, I have watched entrepreneurs trip over the fallacy of complexity. The more complex something is, the more value we believe it must hold. We wrongly assign value to something relative to its complexity when it is the simplest principles—in business and in life—that are always the most valuable.

In this book, Susan has removed the complexity and mythology from entrepreneurship and laid out a series of sound and practical principles and exercises to lead you through the creation or reinvention of your company.

But be forewarned! Just because the principles and exercises contained in this book are simple, by no means are they easy. Entrepreneurship is like giving birth and going to war at the same time. You will labor intensely as you take your idea from concept to reality and then you will wage a daily battle against yourself, your competitors, and the economy at large just to keep your dream alive.

We all need people to fight alongside of us, encourage us, and guide us through the many business battles we will face. Through this book, Susan can do just that. She has labored and fought to bring you these business truths. The result is a book that, should you submit to it, will act as a guide to you as you create a business that fits your wants, needs, and desires—just like your favorite pair of blue jeans.
Summon the courage to dive into this book with all you have and, above all, execute on the ideas laid out."

TRAVIS ROBERTSON
CEO, The Don't Settle Group
travisrobertson.com

"Now and then you discover a book that has you smiling before you are a full chapter in, and then you realize that you have mentally added it to your client holiday gift-giving list because they *must* have a copy. This engaging and inspiring book delivers a potent message about life and business and business and life that will have you raring to craft the best entrepreneurial life that you can possibly envision."

DENISE GRIFFITTS
Web Developer, VA/OBM

"I don't want to spoil your illusions, but I must dispel two rumors about doing business in your blue jeans:
    "It's not as easy as you think."
    "It's not as much fun as you think."
After you read the words of Ms. Baroncini-Moe, you'll see that these are the rumors and what she writes is the truth. Jeans-clad for nearly 60 years, I know her truth to be the one you can take to the bank."

JAY CONRAD LEVINSON
The Father of Guerrilla Marketing
Author of the "Guerrilla Marketing" book series

"Susan's book, *Business in Blue Jeans,* is a valuable resource to anyone trying to get ahead in business without losing their head. It teaches us that we can *be* who we are to *become* who we are."

AMBER OSBORNE
a.k.a. "Miss Destructo"

"Susan demonstrates in this book that you can build a business around the lifestyle you want. *Business in Blue Jeans* provides actionable lessons on everything from mindset to marketing to give the start-up entrepreneur the very best chances of success."

JAMES REYNOLDS
SEO, Sherpa.com

"*Business in Blue Jeans* is a thoughtful, comprehensive guide for anyone who wants to create professional success. Regardless of what you prefer to wear (I go from yoga pants to business suits from one day to the next!), it's about your mindset and what you must do so you're poised to achieve your dreams. Highly recommended!"

FELICIA J. SLATTERY
M.A., M.Ad.Ed., Bestselling author of *21 Ways to Make Money Speaking* and *Kill the Elevator Speech: Stop Selling, Start Connecting*

"This book will make you forget any conventional thoughts about entrepreneurship. A fascinating process that starts by working on your most essential asset—yourself. This is how small businesses are created today."

FRANCISCO ROSALES
SocialMouths.com

BUSINESS in BLUE JEANS

How to Have a Successful Business on Your Own Terms, in Your Own Style

Susan Baroncini-Moe

Sound Wisdom
167 Walnut Bottom Road
Shippensburg, PA 17257

This book and all other Sound Wisdom books are available at bookstores and distributors worldwide.

ISBN 13 TP: 978-1-937879-22-8
ISBN 13 Ebook: 978-1-937879-21-1

For Worldwide Distribution, Printed in the U.S.A.
2 3 4 5 6 7 8 / 17 16 15 14 13

To Leo, who teaches me about life and love every day, and who reminds me to believe.

CONTENTS

PREFACE

When I was a young girl, I was deeply passionate about a dream, and that dream was all about bubble gum. It wasn't the bubble gum itself that I loved, as much as it was *blowing bubbles* with bubble gum. I'd throw an entire pack of gum in my mouth and chew away like a baseball player until the wad was soft enough to start blowing bubbles, and then I'd start blowing the biggest bubbles I could make. There was nothing quite as satisfying as the sound of a really, really good bubble popping.

Luckily for me, my mom was usually pretty good about buying me bubble gum when we went to the store, but sometimes she said no, and if you're six years old and trying to blow the world's largest bubble gum bubble (I had Guinness World Records® aspirations even back then), you have to have bubble gum.

So that was my dream: to keep blowing bubble gum bubbles without interruption. To do that, I knew I needed more money than my allowance, since that money was already going for the essentials (specifically, Barbie clothes, Archie comic books, and Sea Monkeys), and gum was expensive (twenty-five cents a pack!).

One day, after begging my mom to take me to the store to buy another pack of grape Hubba Bubba, I assessed my options. I was only just starting to learn how to play violin, and I still sounded pretty bad, so I knew that wasn't going to help. I wiggled my teeth, but none of them were loose, so the Tooth Fairy was out. Besides, that was only good for a limited time, and I needed something *sustainable*. I was too young to babysit, too young to cut the grass, and I didn't yet have the "mad skillz" my future self would acquire.

It was July. I remember sitting on the sofa in our family room, gazing out the window, daydreaming about bubble gum, when I saw a guy jog past our house. Slowly, it dawned on me. Joggers were *always* going past our house. It was the heyday of the Jim Fixx era. Everybody was jogging.

My dad, a doctor who was friends with the late Jim Fixx, author of *The Complete Book of Running*, had mapped out a two-and-a-half mile route through our neighborhood and passed it out to our neighbors with a title written across the top: "The Moe" (our last name). From that point forward, joggers used that route all the time. To this day, when walkers, joggers, and runners encounter each other in our neighborhood, it's common to ask, "How many 'Moe's have you done today?" In fact, on July 4th, there's an official annual walk and run event in our neighborhood that goes around The Moe.

If you've ever visited the Midwest in July, you know how hot and humid it gets. You probably also know that hydration is key to surviving those "dog days."

Back then, because my dad was such an avid health nut, I'd been to enough walk/run/jog events with my dad to know that every runner loves those tables with cups of Gatorade along the race. And I'd been playing "Lemonade Stand" on my Apple II Plus for a whole year. This was a Hot, Sunny Day, according to the game, which meant it was the perfect time for a lemonade stand, and according to the game dynamics, I could practically charge whatever I wanted!

But...I wasn't sure how to make lemonade. I needed to outsource! I got my mom to make up a batch of grape Kool-Aid (okay, so it wasn't lemonade, precisely, but I was out of the box even back then).

While she was mixing up the Kool-Aid, I curled my hair with a butane curling iron and put on my best velour top and shorts. I dragged my little picnic table out by the street and made up a cardboard sign, and I was in business!

I not only sold out of my Kool-Aid that day, but I sold out of *three* batches. Cars stopped, joggers stopped, friendly neighbors came out to see what I was doing. I delivered every cup with ice and a shy smile, saying, "Thank you so much. Please tell your friends and please come again," or "Thank you for stopping. That was so nice of you. I hope you like your Kool-Aid. I'll be serving cherry flavor tomorrow."

It was glorious, and I had gum without interruption for *the entire summer*. It was my first taste of the power of being an entrepreneur. From that moment on, I was hooked.

Small business is, to me, the essence of the American Dream. Entrepreneurship is the backbone of our economy, and it offers virtually anyone unlimited opportunity, income, and freedom. But like anything worth pursuing, it requires effort.

For some, the effort will be more challenging than for others, by way of circumstance, life path, or lack of skill. I've done what I can in this book to put as much as I can fit into a single volume to give you as much help as I possibly can, and I've put additional resources at the book web site, http://BusinessInBlueJeans.com/book.

It is my greatest hope that this book will give you what you need to start to make your entrepreneurial dreams come true. I'm giving you the tools, the path, and the knowledge to make it happen. Now all you need to do is add some effort and...stir.

INTRODUCTION

YOU ARE NOT ALONE

That's the first thing I want you to know. You are not alone in your small business journey. I decided to write this book because I wanted to reach out to the vast numbers of people starting and growing small businesses and looking for answers to how to create a stable, successful enterprise…in *any* economy.

Right now we're seeing a massive surge in entrepreneurial activity, and millions of people just like you are starting or growing small businesses of all kinds. But starting and growing a business isn't easy, and it won't happen overnight. Anyone who tells you that it is easy and fast is either lying or is trying to sell you something that probably won't help you.

THERE IS NO "GET RICH QUICK" IN BUSINESS

I may have lost you right there. In fact, if you kept reading after that one line, I'm already impressed, so I'll give you a little reward for sticking around: There's more to that sentence!

Ready? Here it is: There is no "get rich quick" in business…but there are *definitely* ways to make the path to success and wealth smoother and faster than if you did it alone.

In this book, I'm going to show you many of the shortcuts I've learned in my years of working with small businesses and entrepreneurs. I'm going to show you what to do and what *not* to do so that you can avoid many of the mistakes that keep businesses from succeeding.

IT'S NEVER TOO LATE

It's never too late to start your business. It's never too late to pursue success. Orville Redenbacher started his popcorn company when he was fifty-eight. Mary Kay Ash was forty-five when she started her cosmetics company. And Colonel Harland Sanders launched Kentucky Fried Chicken with his first Social Security check at age sixty-five.

It is *never* too late to start a business. It is never too late to pursue your dreams. I don't care if you're nine, nineteen, or ninety (well, if you're nine, please get your parents' permission before launching your startup); you can take action *today* and start your business *now*. It is *never* too late. I've worked with clients who are in their twenties and clients who are in their seventies. It doesn't matter how old you are. It matters how much you want to pursue your dreams.

IT DOESN'T MATTER WHERE YOU ARE RIGHT NOW

Whether you're just starting out or you want to grow a business you already have, I'll show you the smartest places to invest your time, energy, and money in your business so that you have the best chance of building that stable, successful business and can lean back and enjoy your life. In each chapter, I'll show you how to apply my principles in very practical ways, regardless of where you are in your business growth.

Plus, I've made this book as close to the experience of working directly with me, one-on-one, as possible. When I work with my clients, I give them "homework assignments," which are practical tasks that they do in between our meetings. Similarly, throughout this book, I'll give you homework assignments to do, and I've designed the assignments so that there are assignments for startups and for businesses in growth. Some exercises are good for just about anyone to do. But where there are differences, look for "Newbies" (for startups) and "Existing Business Owners" (for growing businesses).

So if you're starting a new business, this book's for you. If you've been in business for awhile and want to take your business to the next level, this book's for you, too.

This book will teach you the business fundamentals that far too many businesses don't have in place (don't be so sure yours does, by the way), plus new tricks for your business arsenal.

"WAIT...BUSINESS FUNDAMENTALS? PFFT! I NEED ADVANCED HELP!"

Let me take a moment here to make a case for business fundamentals. All too often, business owners and entrepreneurs *think* they have the basics worked out. I see it all the time, and it comes in many forms.

For example, a coach comes to me for help growing her new practice, and in our first meeting, when I'm analyzing the business and which areas I think will yield the best return on the investment of our time and attention, when I ask about the name of her business and where it came from, she says, "It's a name that's really meaningful to me." That response tells me she's skipped some fundamentals, like knowing her target market and designing a brand that appeals to the people she most wants to work with.

Then there's the corporate executive who comes to me and wants to know why he's having a hard time getting repeat customers, and during my analysis, I discover that his customer service line keeps people on hold for lengthy periods of time and his customer service representatives are lackadaisical. That tells me he's missing some of the fundamentals, like knowing what real service to customers is and understanding how employee engagement transfers to customer loyalty.

The fundamentals of business are the foundation of everything we do. There's a reason why they're fundamentals. They're the basic principles that have stood the test of time. The fundamentals don't change. Strategies and tactics change, but the fundamentals don't.

And if you think, *Come on, I've heard all of this before,* it's a sure sign that you need to hear it again, because you probably haven't opened yourself up to the knowledge and taken it in.

The reason I talk about the fundamentals is threefold:

1. Newbies and startups need to learn them,

2. Existing businesses still aren't getting it and need to hear it, and

3. If you don't have the fundamentals in place, then ultimately, you're going to be chasing anything that you think might work to grow your business, making you easy prey for scam artists and con men peddling the next, latest, greatest "magic bullet" tactic that can change the course of your business and make you the next millionaire. Trust me, there's *no* single strategy or tactic that can do that for your business.

What builds success is creating a stable, strong business that's based on fundamental principles and then fusing that solid foundation with the best-performing strategies that apply to your business and your target market. That's what I'm going to teach you in this book.

MY STYLE, MY WAY VS. YOUR STYLE, YOUR WAY

When I came up with the idea of "Business in Blue Jeans," it was, in part, because I wanted to roll up my sleeves and work in the trenches with my clients and their businesses. I personally work best when I'm comfortable and when I'm not distracted by uncomfortable clothes. So yes, I often work in my jeans.

But there's more to the story. Business in Blue Jeans is also a metaphor. Think about your favorite pair of jeans—that pair that's worn in all the right places and fits perfectly, the pair that makes you look ten pounds lighter. When you wear those jeans, don't you feel good about yourself? That's how I want you to feel about your business. I want your business to fit you perfectly and to show you in the best possible light.

I also want your business to have the characteristics of denim. I want it to be strong, stable, and lasting. That's what a Business in Blue Jeans is really all about.

So it's not about wearing jeans to work every day. That's *my* style. Your style might be different. That's okay. You can wear a suit to work and still have a Business in Blue Jeans.

My business is structured so that I can travel regularly and work from anywhere in the world, whether it's in the heart of urban Montevideo, Uruguay (where I worked on the outline for this book) or the English countryside (where I wrote this chapter) or a vineyard in Tuscany (where I drank a lot of wine and ate far too much pasta), or in my comfortable home office in Indianapolis (which I share with three hamsters, and where I wrote the bulk of the book). That's *my* dream. That's *my* way of doing business. Your way of doing business might be completely different. That's okay, too.

This book isn't about how to copycat my business model or any kind of one-size-fits-all marketing strategies. It's about how to develop and grow a business that suits you, fits your values, and creates the kind of lifestyle you want to create for yourself and your family, using business fundamentals that have stood the test of time.

WHAT YOU CAN EXPECT

I don't pull my punches. I'm going to give it to you straight. And often, just like with my clients, I'm going to give you homework assignments throughout this book. You'll do these exercises independently, outside of the book. I recommend using a notebook or creating a document file to type your answers into, but if you prefer to do them in a fancier, official workbook, there's one for most every chapter, available for you to download at http://BusinessInBlueJeans .com/book.

BRAIN JUNK

BRAIN JUNK

Entrepreneurs get tripped up in *many* ways. When you think about all the business mistakes people can make, you may think about things like not having a good business plan or not having enough capital to finance your endeavor. (By the way, while this book doesn't cover how to fund your business, the bonus content on the book web site does: http://BusinessInBlueJeans.com/book.) You might think about poor branding or bad marketing strategies.

You might not realize that a business can get derailed before it even gets started just because of what I call "brain junk."

Brain junk is the mental baggage that gets in your way, and it can stop you from having a successful business *before you've even started it.*

If you've ever thought, *I want to start a business, but I can't because I'm not smart enough, and I don't know anything about business,* or *I want to grow my business, but I can't because I don't have enough money,* or *My business hasn't grown, and it must be because I'm not good enough,* then you have some brain junk. If you've ever wondered why other people seem to be able to create successful businesses while you flounder, then you have some brain junk. And we're going to handle the brain junk before we get into the nuts and bolts of your business.

THE ONE FACTOR I CAN'T ACCOUNT FOR

I can teach you everything I know about business (but probably not in the space I'm allowed for this book). I can give you the information about business models and branding and marketing and social media and customer service. I can teach you how to network and I can show you how to assemble a team. I can show you all the keys to success.

The one factor I can't account for, though, is you. I don't know what you've experienced in your lifetime. I don't know what you learned growing up. I don't know what your work ethic is. I don't know how confident you are.

So while I can give you everything you need to be successful in business, the only ingredient I can't account for is you, and that means that your success is really, ultimately up to you.

DON'T SKIP THIS STUFF!

Early in my career, occasionally I would get a client who was emphatically against working on the personal elements. These clients wanted to jump into branding and marketing their businesses because they thought the nuts and bolts pieces were the most important things they needed.

> **A business can get derailed before it even gets started just because of "brain junk."**

That's when I discovered that entrepreneurs who skip the Brain Junk Step often end up creating businesses that don't bring them joy, thinking too small, branding for the short term, and getting stuck pretty quickly. In fact, willingness to work on your brain junk is a good indicator for whether you'll be successful or not.

Working through the brain junk now means that you can sort out the voices in your head and get absolute clarity on what's in your heart. It means that you can open yourself up to all the things you've never allowed yourself to dream about or hope for in life and start seeing those things as possible. It means that you can change how you see yourself so that you can walk taller and feel stronger. It means that you can learn to deal with self-doubt and fear—intermittent companions for most entrepreneurs—so that you conquer them, and not the other way around.

And it means that you can think much bigger about what you want to create so that you can create a *business* instead of just a job for yourself. Working through the brain junk also means that you'll be more productive and creative, so you'll do better work in the long run.

Here's the really big secret most successful entrepreneurs don't want you to know: Even the most successful people in the world experience self-doubt. I've experienced my own mindset issues throughout my career. I know that most of my colleagues have too. If you've listened to my interviews, you've heard me ask everyone from celebrity entrepreneurs, bestselling authors, well-known public speakers, and experts about their brain junk and how they dealt with it. Everybody has it.

What sets really successful people apart from everyone else is that we work on our brain junk so that nothing stands in our way. Aside from being afraid of what you might find, there is no downside to working through the brain junk. And since ninety-nine percent of the clients I've worked with over the years have had some brain junk to work out, I'm guessing that you do too. In fact, it might very well be the thing that's holding you back. So let's deal with it and then move on to the nuts and bolts.

"GRASSHOPPER MODE"

There's a story in the Bible about the children of Israel who, upon reaching the Promised Land, were afraid to enter. The verse says, "And there we saw the giants and we were in our own sight as grasshoppers, and so we were in their sight" (Num. 13:33 KJV).

This "grasshopper mode" is something that happens to everyone. We see the "giants" in our field and think of ourselves as grasshoppers. But we've *all* been grasshoppers at one time or another. And more importantly, we're all grasshoppers compared to somebody with more experience or expertise.

Bravo! has a cooking competition show for aspiring chefs called *Top Chef*. Throughout the competition, young professionals competing on the show encounter the best chefs in the world as the master chefs come to judge various competitions. You can see how star-struck the aspiring chefs are. You can literally see them shift into grasshopper mode, where they see themselves as small and the master chefs as giants.

After a few seasons of *Top Chef,* Bravo! created a new series called *Top Chef Masters,* in which the best chefs in the world compete for donations to charitable causes in the same kinds of competitions as the young professional chefs endure in the regular series.

What's fascinating about the *Top Chef Masters* series isn't the mastery of the cooking, but rather the experience of the giants of the culinary world. Going through this competition and being challenged in new ways humbles the chefs, and the audience gets to see them experience quite a bit of self-doubt and fear. They become the grasshoppers.

So you see, we're all grasshoppers and we're all giants.

Here's where it gets *really* interesting. Going back to that verse, "And there we saw the giants and we were in our own sight as grasshoppers, *and so we were in their sight"* (Num. 13:33 KJV). When you see yourself as a grasshopper, you essentially teach others how to see you. You put off a "vibe" that tells people that you see yourself as a grasshopper and that you *are* a grasshopper.

See yourself as small and insignificant, and others will see you that way, too. But see yourself as someone important, as someone who's on the verge of being hugely successful, and that's how the world will see you.

If you see yourself as a grasshopper though, it's not so easy to start seeing yourself as a giant. And even giants have their grasshopper days. Successful people experience fear and doubt and mindset issues *all the time,* just like you do. We just know what to do about it. I'm going to share the strategies we use with you in this chapter.

THE MINDSET FACTOR

Mindset matters because your mindset—where your head is—guides everything else. Your mindset guides how well you can "think big," how much you believe in your ability to succeed, how well you can think creatively and outside the box, and whether you can really stick with this and stay motivated. Mindset, in short, is everything.

You know how time can pass slowly or quickly depending on what you're doing or how you're feeling? Well, that's mindset. And you know how you can find it easy to accomplish certain goals, while others are a struggle? That's mindset, too.

Also, if your mindset is all junked up with limitations about who you are and what you can accomplish, you'll be finished before you even start.

As children we dream of being astronauts, rocket scientists. Do you remember? What did *you* dream about? Was it going to the moon, fighting fires, flying in the air? As children, there's absolutely nothing holding us back.

But as we grow, we develop ideas about who we are and what we're capable of. People tell us we're not good enough or we can't do certain things. We're told we need to be realistic, and when we incorporate these statements into our psyche, they turn into beliefs about who we are and what we can accomplish; they become "limiting beliefs."

As we incorporate these limiting beliefs into who we are, we begin to forget our dreams or to minimize our successes and "put things into perspective." We make our dreams smaller so we don't have to deal with disappointment. We keep quiet about what we wish for so that people don't call us dreamers.

What's Wrong With Being a Dreamer?

Whoa, hold on. What's wrong with being a dreamer? Is it really so bad to be a dreamer? No, it's not.

When people use *dreamer* as a derogatory term, there's usually a reason for it. Maybe they've seen people they care about go after a dream, only to fall short. Maybe they themselves had dreams and ambitions that were never realized.

People who don't know how to go after their dreams or who have experienced failure often call others dreamers when they want to bring them back down to Earth and remind them what the "real world" is like. It's not necessarily malicious. Sometimes it's just a misguided attempt to protect people they care about.

But what if you *never* put your dreams away? What if you never let anyone tell you what your limitations are? What would be possible? As Robert Schuller famously said, *"What would you attempt to do if you knew you could not fail?"*

Take a moment, right now, to close your eyes and sit with this question. What would *you* attempt to do if you knew you couldn't fail? What if you could let your light shine as bright as it can shine without the possibility of being dimmed by any shade? Sit with that. Ponder it.

HOMEWORK ASSIGNMENT:
THE LIST OF 100

The first step to re-opening yourself to your dreams and accessing all that's possible is to make The List of 100. The List of 100 is a way to reactivate the dreamer in you. You're going to make a list of one hundred things that you want in life. It can be material things; it can be a certain income level, places you want to travel, experiences you want to have...it can be whatever you want.

If you get to fifty and get stuck, take a little time away and then go back and start writing again. Keep working until you get to one hundred and make this a living, breathing document that you update regularly. If you get really stuck, it's time to start looking at the voices in your head and what's holding you back from discovering what you really want.

HOMEWORK ASSIGNMENT:
THE "DREAM TO REALITY BOOK"

This next exercise is based on the life coaching "Wheel of Life," which is a tool coaches use for helping clients quantify their level of satisfaction with various areas of their lives. Using the categories from that tool (plus a few of my own), I've developed this "Dream to Reality" exercise.

First, create the right environment by following these steps:

1. Close your eyes.

2. See yourself at your highest peak of success, a point where you've achieved everything you've always dreamed of (and even some stuff you haven't yet imagined).

3. Step into the body of that successful version of yourself (or, if you have a hard time imagining yourself at this point, imagine someone who you know who has achieved the level of success you want and step into their body).

4. What does it feel like to be this version of yourself? How do you stand? What is your posture like? How confident do you feel?

In that mindset, as the most successful version of yourself, begin to create your "Dream to Reality Book," in which you write down the greatest, coolest things you have accomplished at this point in your life, at this moment when you've reached your pinnacle of success.

Write in the present tense, as in, "My books are New York Times bestsellers, and I have had both a non-fiction business book and a novel on the bestseller list." (Yes, that's an example from my own book.)

Your "Dream to Reality Book" has eight chapters:

Chapter 1: Business

Start with an inventory of the awards, honors, and cool recognitions that you've received. Include a description of your professional support team and your work environment. Write about who you serve and how you serve them, how you spend your time, and what your day looks like.

Chapter 2: Family and Friends

In this chapter, you'll write about your relationships. Describe the quality of these relationships and how you spend your time with the people in your life.

Chapter 3: Environment

Here you'll write about your home environment. Describe how it looks and feels and is maintained.

Chapter 4: Time Management

This chapter is about how you balance your time. How do you spend your days?

Chapter 5: Contribution/Spirituality

This section is about your contribution to the world as well as your personal spiritual practice.

Chapter 6: Health

Here you'll write about your physical health and how you maintain and take care of your body.

Chapter 7: Personal Support Team

This is an inventory of the people who support you in your personal life. This list might include coaches, counselors, attorneys who handle personal matters, financial advisors, friends, housekeepers, etc.

Chapter 8: Wealth

This is the inventory of your material things, such as cars, homes around the world, jewels, investment accounts, and charitable donations.

What Comes Next

Once you've completed your "Dream to Reality Book," take some time to meditate on what you've written. Get inside those dreams and feel what it feels like to have already achieved each one. And then...put that book away.

Contrary to what you'll read in many personal growth and motivational books, I *don't* recommend that you review these goals every day. At the most, review your goals once a week or even once a month. Set aside a time that you meditate on your dreams just that one time each week and then *move on.*

Your goals and dreams *are* important. However, you don't necessarily want to get so wrapped up in those written-in-present-tense goals that you live inside of them, essentially living in the future rather than doing the work of the moment.

Sometimes people get so focused on their grand ambitions that they can only see the future, not the path they need to take to get to that future. As a result, they often end up stagnating and spending most of their time in unproductive fantasizing, under the delusion that they're somehow using the Law of Attraction to bring their dreams to life.

There's nothing wrong with dreaming, but you can't dream things into reality. You have to put in some elbow grease to make things happen.

Sometimes people get so tied up in their present-tense dreams that they expect to already be at the point where they actually *have* achieved those dreams, and they can't understand why other people aren't seeing it. This can lead to inappropriately large egos, looking for shortcuts to take the easy route to success, and a chaotic, scattershot approach to success.

And while there's nothing inherently wrong with honorable shortcuts (*not* shortcuts that make use of shady or illicit marketing tactics, for example), it's exceedingly rare for someone to be so incredibly brilliant and amazing that

> **You can't dream things into reality. You have to put in some elbow grease to make them happen.**

that he or she gets to jump the line. Even overnight successes rarely actually happen overnight.

So write out your goals and dreams and ambitions, and write them in present tense. But once you do that, set them aside and just focus on *the work*.

The Voices in Your Head

Have you ever taken a moment to notice all the voices in your head? While you're going about your daily life, there are voices in your head that are observing, considering, judging, commenting on the past, planning for the future, making lists, reacting to everything...it's an almost endless dialogue. And only *some* of the voices in your head belong to you.

That's right. You have voices in your head that belong to all kinds of people: family members, friends, teachers, pastors, bosses, coworkers, some random person that you met at a bar one time. They're all in there, they all have something to say, and we all make the mistake of thinking that what *they're* saying is what *we* believe.

For example, I once had a client who believed that he didn't have what it took to be successful. He simply could not believe that he could do anything that would contribute to his own success. As we worked on this piece of his brain junk, he realized that all his life, whenever something really good happened to him, his father would tell him that he was "lucky." Over time, he incorporated his father's voice into his own thinking so that every time something good happened, instead of believing that his success was his own hard work and efforts paying off, he believed it was just luck.

When we uncovered this truth and he identified that voice in his head as his father voice, and not his own voice, his confidence and belief in himself grew, and he was able to see his own efforts as worthwhile and integral to creating his future success.

The voices in our heads tell us all kinds of information, and the information they provide is often just flat-out wrong. I grew up believing that my own success made others feel small. I learned to keep my accomplishments small and never put in much effort so that I lived in a kind of limbo all the time.

Then one day, as I was doing some of this work myself, I realized that the voice telling me that my greatness hurt other people was absolutely *not* my own voice. Not long after that epiphany, I was swinging life around by the tail. Since then, I've accomplished some pretty big things, including breaking a Guinness World Record.

The voices in your head sometimes tell you that you shouldn't want things. You shouldn't wish for more than you have. In fact, sometimes the voices in your head say that you should just be grateful for what you have and not want more. *It is absolutely okay to be grateful for what you have* and *to still want more.*

As you make your way through this book and begin to grow your business, you're likely to hear some of those voices piping up. Most likely, they'll discourage you and you'll experience some anxiety or fear. It happens to the best of us, so I feel pretty comfortable telling you that it's likely to come up at least some time along the way in your entrepreneurial journey.

When the voices in your head pop up and start to make you doubt yourself, take a moment and let the voices tell you what their *real* message is. Most of the time, these messages come from well-intentioned people who care about us.

A discouraging message may sound like "This business is a foolish idea," but might actually just be saying, "I don't want to see you experience pain."

Sometimes these messages come from people who are envious, and in those cases, a message that seems discouraging and sounds like, "I can't believe you'd try to do something like that," might actually be saying, "I wish I had your guts," or "I wish I could dream the way that you do," or "I wish I had your talents, skills, or abilities."

And sometimes the messages come from people who are just mean. Those messages might sound like, "You'll never be a success," and are usually, "I hurt, so I want others to hurt, because I believe that will make me hurt less."

Your job is threefold here:

1. Determine whose voices are in your head and discover the consistent messages they send you.

2. Translate the message into what it's *really* trying to tell you.

3. Decide if you want to heed the message or ignore it. If you heed it, it'll become *your* voice. If you ignore it, you'll start to replace it with a different message (that's coming up).

That's it. It's not always easy to go through the process, but once you begin to identify the voices, you'll automatically find yourself questioning them whenever they come up.

Replacing Negative Thoughts

When you discover that the voices in your head have some messages that don't resonate with who you are or who you want to be, that's the time to start replacing the messages.

Sometimes the negative thoughts that you have are echoes from the past—things that you heard someone say that stuck with you, either because what was said really hurt at the time or because the words were repeated again and again.

Sometimes negative thoughts are what you believe about yourself, things that simply are not true, but because you've gotten in the habit of repeating them in your head, you think they are true.

Whatever they are, wherever they came from, to be successful and avoid sabotaging yourself or thinking too small (or whatever your particular brain junk is), you must develop a way of managing negative thoughts so that they don't rule your mind.

HOMEWORK ASSIGNMENT:
POSITIVE EQUIVALENTS

The first step toward replacing negative thoughts is to write them down. Write them down for an entire day—two days, if necessary. Keep a log of all the negative thoughts you have throughout the day. Don't worry about how many there are and don't judge yourself for having negative thoughts. Just observe how many you have and write them all down.

When you've completed that step, look over your list and see if you can organize the negative thoughts that you've recorded into categories. What patterns can you find in the negative thoughts that you experience on a daily basis?

Next, start to write the positive equivalent for each negative thought. So, if your recurring negative thought is, "I don't have what it takes to be successful," then your positive equivalent is something like, "I'm learning the skills to become more successful." And we know that's true, by the way, because you're reading this book.

I've had multiple clients who, when they did this exercise, told me that they realized one of their patterns was, "I don't know how to grow a business," but they quickly discovered that their positive equivalent was, "I'm learning how to grow a business."

Other Tools and Strategies

There are many other tools and strategies that may be useful for you. Among them are affirmations, vision boards, and meditation.

I'm a big fan of meditation, but I've had clients that can't get into it and don't find it helpful. I have some clients who love affirmations and some who can't stand them. As for vision boards, some clients of mine use magazines and newspapers to create real boards they hang on a wall of their office, while others use a site like Pinterest to collate and create a digital vision board.

These tools are all about creating a system that works best for you. Experiment with all the homework assignments and tools and see what resonates with you and your unique personality.

CREATING THE SUCCESS MINDSET

Once you've started the process of replacing your negative thoughts, it's time to start getting into the success mindset—to start really opening up your brain and thinking like a successful person.

HOMEWORK ASSIGNMENT:
INVENTORY OF SUCCESS

Your Inventory of Success is a document where you curate your lifetime of achievements. You simply list all the awesome stuff you've done in your lifetime. I keep mine in an online document so that I can update it each time something cool happens.

You can start back as far as you want to go. I started with age five and included things like having won a grade school pumpkin-carving contest. Even if you tried something and it didn't go the way that you thought it should have, it can be considered a success. For example, in my Inventory of Success, I include the number of times I've asked Seth Godin for an interview. He turns me down every time. But one day I know he'll say yes, so I consider my persistence a success: Seth! E-mail me! Let's talk!

Include everything you can think of, and if you start to get stuck, ask people who know you and your history for help. I once sent out an e-mail to my family and closest friends and asked them to recall five of my accomplishments or successes. That turned out to be a cool exercise for many reasons, not the least of which is that I saw that my family thinks I'm awesome.

Make sure your Inventory of Success is a living document that you continue to add to. Every time you do something amazing, every time you get a testimonial, every time you go out on a limb, put it in the Inventory.

Planning Your "Whys"

I take a different approach to business than you may be used to. I've always thought that it makes sense to know what your goals in life are first, so that when you construct your business, you think in terms of business models that have the most potential to help you reach those goals.

For example, let's say that you have expensive taste. Let's say that you want to own a house in the south of France, a horse ranch in Montana, and a mansion in Malibu. You want a boat, an expensive sports car, and a couture wardrobe. If that's the case, you're going to need a different business model than someone who has much more modest needs.

That's why I started having my clients map out their dreams and goals. Each of us has a different idea of what success means. If you get clear on what *your* definition of success is, then you can create a business that matches up with your unique values.

Planning your whys means making a list of reasons why you do what you do. Let's get real here: You don't really want to sell widgets or work with clients. What you *really* want is that house in France or to buy that fancy car or to pet a tiger (one of my personal dreams). What I want is to sit on the sofa with my husband at night watching *So You Think You Can Dance* and eating popcorn with money in the bank.

Those are the whys.

HOMEWORK ASSIGNMENT:
PLANNING YOUR WHYS

Start making your list now. What are your dreams? Get really specific here and start attaching dollar figures to each thing that you list. Want a Ducati motorcycle? Write it down.

Then spend a few minutes finding out about how much that motorcycle costs and write that down. Want to have a retirement fund with $2,000,000 in it? Write it down.

Create a "Why" budget, too. Just like you'd plan out how much you need for mortgage, utilities, food, "fun money," and monthly spa visits (or whatever), create a budget for your dream lifestyle.

For a list of resources to help you find the cost of things and a tool to help you create your "Why Budget," visit http://BusinessInBlueJeans.com/book.

Now that you have a sense of how much cash you need to create your dream lifestyle, you're better equipped to choose a business model. We'll get to that in a couple of chapters.

Sometimes my clients are shocked by how much their dream lifestyle could cost. I've also had a few clients who were surprised to learn that what they wanted in life cost far less than they expected. But when you start planning your whys, you start to get clear about the goals you're after, and you can plan your real business in a practical, quantifiable, results-oriented way.

Equally important, in writing down these dreams and starting to put a dollar figure to each one, you make them much more real. The more tangible and real your dreams feel to you, the more motivating they'll be. This is what you're working toward—what your business will make possible in your life! It's fun and exciting stuff!

The Why Aftermath

An interesting phenomenon occurs with many of my clients after they do the "Planning Your Whys" exercise.

Some clients are excited and motivated by the exercise. But others see that their dreams are expensive—I don't care what the economic climate is, houses in Malibu don't come cheap—and start to get nervous. Those voices in their head come back, saying things like, *Who do you think you are? You can't make that kind of money!* and *You should be grateful for what you have. Why do you need all that stuff?*

Fairly quickly, they start to pull back from their dreams and begin to try to be more "realistic." They begin editing themselves and squashing those big dreams back down.

This is usually the point where we start to get to the heart of your mindset issues. So get ready.

Authenticity and Your Real Story

We all tell stories about ourselves—to others and to ourselves. But the stories you tell yourself aren't always the same as the stories you tell the world, are they? You want the world to see you a certain way, but that's not always the way that you see yourself.

Successful people know how to get honest with their stories and make

> **Even if you think you're hiding it, your true story will show up in your business.**

sure they're telling authentic stories to the world and to themselves. That means the story you tell yourself has to be the same as the story you tell the world. It all has to be *authentic*.

If you don't get your stories in harmony, they're going to clash, and ultimately, two things will happen: 1) You'll be found out, and 2) your progress toward your dreams will be threatened.

When you're not telling the same stories to the world that you're telling yourself about who you are and what you're capable of, the disharmony pervades every aspect of your life.

Ask yourself if you're being authentic. Are you being honest about your story—who you are, what you've experienced, and where you are today?

This is a time to get *really* honest. What's your story? What are you trying to hide from? What don't you want other people to know? You want to get to the heart of this, because sure enough, even if you think you're hiding it, your story, your *true* story, will show up in the way that *you* show up, in your business, in your interaction with clients, and in your sales process.

For example, if you're desperate to pay your bills, you don't want to show that in your business. You'll *try* to look successful, but ultimately, without you even realizing it, you'll probably show up as desperate to make a sale. If your true story and the story you tell the world don't coincide, the truth will shine through, even when you think it won't. So get clear about what your story is, *especially* the parts you're hiding from, and turn that story around so it works for you, not against you.

HOMEWORK ASSIGNMENT:
WHAT'S YOUR TRUE STORY?

Answer the following:

1. What's the story that you tell others about yourself?

2. What's your true story?

3. Are these stories the one and the same?

4. What do you most want to hide from?

5. What don't you want other people to know about you?

6. What are you most afraid of?

7. Are there any stories of failure that you're hiding from? And if so, how can you transform those stories into a learning moment?

The Big Stretch

One thing truly successful entrepreneurs know is that you have to get comfortable with being uncomfortable. I call this The Big Stretch.

You know how, at the gym, when you first start to stretch, it hurts a lot and you can really feel that pull? The more you stretch, the less it hurts and the easier it gets, so you stretch a little more until you feel the pull again.

That's what it's like to be a successful entrepreneur. You constantly do things that challenge you and make you stretch a little so you can see your limitations...until you get used to them and have to push the boundaries a little further.

It can be a little scary to be an entrepreneur and to be stretching all the time like this. But if you're born to be an entrepreneur, that stretch will feel a little bit good and a little bit exciting, too.

Not long ago, I was pretty nervous about doing webinars and video interviews. In fact, whenever I did a video, I spent a lot of time working to get my hair and makeup *just right* and recorded an embarrassingly large number of takes to get the perfect video. I would work on a script, practice it over and over and over...I had almost no confidence in myself on video.

> ❝ **Successful people do things that make them feel uncomfortable because those are the things that keep their businesses growing.** ❞

Then I decided to host a webcast to break the Guinness World Records® record for the world's longest uninterrupted live webcast, and spent two days on camera. Talk about a stretch!

If you watch the playback of the webcast (it's available at http://breakarecordwithsusan.com) you can see my nerves in the first hour or so. But as the event progressed, I got more and more comfortable with being on camera, and now I do videos and webcasts regularly and it's not at all scary for me.

Successful people keep stretching and doing things that make them feel uncomfortable because these are the things that keep their businesses growing. So start getting comfortable with The Big Stretch.

Finding "Your Happy Place"

This is one of the last exercises I'm going to give you in this chapter. I started calling it the "happy place" years ago, somewhat cavalierly, because I think it's funny to say "Go to your happy place." But this is actually a useful, serious tool that you can use.

HOMEWORK ASSIGNMENT:
FINDING YOUR HAPPY PLACE

Create a clear vision of what would make you the absolute happiest in life. Write out a full description of what that looks and feels like for you.

Your description can be a place, but it can also be a moment in time. For example, my happy place is when my husband wraps his arms around me and I have a feeling of absolute safety and love.

The feeling I experience in that moment in time is my "happy place." Yours might be a place that you love or a moment from your past.

Whatever your happy place is, what's most important is that every night when you go to bed, you close your eyes and "go to your happy place." Create a powerfully positive image in your mind, right before you drift off to sleep. Doing this allows you to sleep through the night. That same powerfully positive image allows you to wake up in the morning with an optimistic, faith-filled attitude with which you can conquer your day.

WHEN IT'S TIME TO FIND HELP

There are times when the exercises and homework assignments I've given you aren't enough. Sometimes the brain junk is big enough that you'll want to seek out help to address it. Counselors, therapists, coaches—they're all great assets when you need to move forward in your life and don't want to be hindered by brain junk. If you need help, get it.

If you can't afford to hire someone to help you, if coaching is out of reach at the moment, then find someone else who's in the same boat and coach each other honestly. Or think outside the box and make a coach an offer.

I've had people say, "Hey, I can't afford to work with you one-on-one by phone every week, but what if I wanted to e-mail you with questions now and again? Or what if I wanted to call you once a month, or once every other month?" Many coaches and consultants like people who think outside the box and get creative. We're here to help. Don't be afraid to ask for help if you need it.

TAKING CARE OF YOURSELF

Successful entrepreneurship requires more than just the right mindset. Your mindset, obviously, is tied to your brain. And your brain is part of your body. For your brain to work at optimum levels, you have to take care of your body. You also need a lot of energy to run a business, so taking good care of yourself is critical to your success.

Remember: You are your most valuable resource. Take care of yourself!

Sleep

Taking care of yourself starts with getting enough sleep. When you don't get enough sleep or enough *good* sleep, you can have memory problems, depression, and a weakened immune system (so you get sick more). If you think you can solve the problem by drinking more coffee, think again. Caffeine can't overcome a lack of good sleep.

How Much Sleep?

We're all wired a little differently in terms of how much sleep we need. Generally, seven to eight hours is good, but some people can get away with five, while others require ten. Determine what works best for you and stick with it.

Try to get up at the same time every morning. Sleeping in on weekends is a bad idea because it messes up your circadian rhythms—the built-in biological clock that determines all kinds of stuff about your body.

" You are your most valuable resource. Take care of yourself! "

I get up at the same time every day religiously, no matter what day it is. For the most part, in order to keep my hours regulated, I don't consume any caffeine past 5:00 p.m., and I don't eat after 7:00 p.m.; otherwise, I'll be up later than I intend and will ultimately pay the price by waking up later the next day. The only times when my schedule changes are when the seasons (and thus, the light/dark cycle) change or when I'm traveling.

Sleep Tips

Invest in a good quality mattress. Many people have a hard time sleeping because they have a poor mattress. My husband, Leo, and I tried all kinds of mattresses, researched the subject for months, and drove to Chicago to test some hard-to-find brands before choosing ours. In a mattress, you want support, comfort, and space, *and* if you sleep with someone else, you want to make sure you can't feel them moving around, which is a big source of sleep disruption.

Our mattress is my greatest creature comfort and something we really invested in. (Heck, if you're spending twenty-five to thirty percent of your life in a bed, you *should* invest in it!) Whenever I travel, I can't wait to get home to my bed. Other than my niece and nephew, that bed is the one thing I miss most when Leo and I are away from home.

Don't take naps. Even though studies have shown that naps really don't harm your sleep cycle in general and *can* reduce stress and even improve productivity, I'm not a big fan of naps, even when I'm recovering from jet lag. I find that when I take a nap, I'm not as sleepy when it's time for me to go to bed. So I avoid naps whenever possible.

No alcohol before bed. Alcohol may make you feel relaxed and sleepy initially, but it can cause you to have fragmented sleep.

Make your bedroom restful. Your bedroom should be a place of peace and relaxation. It's hard to sleep well in a room that's cluttered and chaotic, so keep your bedroom tidy and clean. Make your bedroom a sanctuary that's all about peace and quiet.

Some people suggest adding blackout shades to your windows, but I find them confusing. I hate waking up in a blackened room and not being able to tell what time it is. I wake up with the sunlight, and that helps me to feel refreshed. You might find that blackout shades work well for you. Experiment and find out what works best.

Most articles on sleep tell you not to watch TV or read in bed. I think that's a bunch of hooey. Leo and I don't watch shows that are too brain-stimulating, but we love watching TV in bed at night. Also, I love reading in bed and find it enormously relaxing. So do what works best for you here as well.

Cool down your bedroom. Studies have shown that dropping your body temperature a little bit helps make you drowsy. That's one reason that taking a hot bath before bedtime helps you sleep better—it's not raising your body temperature that helps you sleep, but the drop in temperature *after* the bath that makes you sleepy. Similarly, a cooler bedroom will help you sleep better.

Exercise

In addition to being a great strategy to improve the quality of your sleep, exercise is important for all kinds of other things, too. Exercise is a great stress reliever and of course, it's good for your overall health. But did you know that exercise can actually improve your mood, boost energy, and ward off things like stroke, type 2 diabetes, depression, certain types of cancer, arthritis, and falls? Exercise even helps your brain to work better by increasing certain chemicals that create new brain cells and form new connections that help you learn.

What's really interesting is that we now know that if you work in a sedentary job (one where you're sitting most of the time), you're at a higher risk for obesity, type 2 diabetes, hypertension, cardiovascular disease, and certain kinds of cancer. You'd think that stopping at the gym for an hour-long workout would mitigate that risk, but I've read several studies that indicate that it doesn't work that way.

Reading this research scared me enough that I started using a treadmill desk, which is a desk that fits over a treadmill. You can get pre-built treadmill desks (they're usually super expensive), or you can build your own (my husband built mine, and you can see photos of it on my blog at http://susanbaroncini-moe.com).

You'd be surprised at just how easy it is to get used to standing up while you work and walking while you work. Even walking at a slow pace is better than sitting down all the time. I've discovered that when I'm working on the treadmill desk, my energy stays constant throughout the day, and I'm far more productive than when I'm sitting at a traditional desk.

What's most important, though, is that you get some exercise in most days and that you *sweat*, even if you're doing yoga.

Nutrition

I'm not an expert in nutrition, but I do know that it's critical to feed your body and your brain the best foods possible so that you can operate at peak efficiency and have sustained, consistent energy throughout the day. That means it's time to evaluate your diet and what you consume. Do you live on junk food and fast food? Does everything in your diet come out of a box, a can, or some other kind of package?

Every nutritionist I've ever spoken to has said that the best diet is broad and varied and includes a large number of extremely colorful fresh foods. I try to stick to that as much as possible, but I've been known to consume my fair share of chocolate and crispy snacks from time to time. Nobody's perfect.

Hydration is also extremely important. I start every day with a big glass of cold water and keep drinking water throughout my day.

Stress

Stress can wreak all kinds of havoc on your mind and body. It can keep you from being able to think clearly and can interfere with your ability to plan your business wisely. Stress can also cause health problems. These days everyone's talking about the "mind-body connection," and we now know that stress takes a physical toll on your body.

Stress comes from all kinds of places, but wherever your stress comes from, it's critical that you learn how to minimize what you can and manage the rest.

The best ways that I've found to help manage my stress are exercise (particularly yoga) and meditation. I wasn't a big believer in meditation at first, but once I started incorporating it into my daily routine, I discovered that I was able to quiet all the "noise" in my mind so that I could work much more effectively and find solutions to problems quickly.

In fact, I credit yoga and meditation with being one of my greatest assets when I was attempting to break the Guinness World Records® title for the world's longest uninterrupted live webcast. During this thirty-six-hour event, I coordinated thirty-four speakers on three continents, seven witnesses, an online event and a live in-person event with audio and video. Plus, I conducted seven interviews and did two presentations, three live question-and-answer sessions, and one live business makeover hour. I also emceed most of the event. *And* I planned the entire event in fifty-five days.

Two days before the event, two speakers and a witness pulled out of the event, plus a few presenters needed to move their times around. I was approving signage, programs, and sponsor logos, testing equipment, training presenters on the webcast technology.

Looking back, I was surprised that I was as calm as I was in the middle of what everyone else would have called a tornado of activity. Hosting *any* live event is stressful, but hosting an event with this many moving parts has the potential to be epically stressful.

But because I started each day with a yoga practice and meditation (even if it was just fifteen minutes long), my stress was minimized, allowing me to handle problems quickly and efficiently and move on to the next thing. I even managed to cook my husband dinner every night leading up to the event. (But don't give me sainthood yet—the poor man is lucky he's Spanish and Italian and can cook up a storm, because otherwise he'd starve while I'm writing this book!)

Experiment with exercise, yoga, and meditation, and find what works best for you. On the web site for this book (http://BusinessInBlueJeans .com/book), I've listed my favorite resources.

Time Management

One of the biggest challenges for any entrepreneur, especially the *micro-entrepreneur* (a term I coined to refer to entrepreneurs who are just starting out and/or run businesses with fewer than twenty employees), is finding enough time to get everything done.

Time is a *huge* factor for entrepreneurs. If you want to be successful, you need *time*. You need time to come up with ideas, figure out how to develop and launch them, and then implement your plans.

When you're first starting out, you may be doing most things yourself for awhile. So it's quite common to be overwhelmed. There are many ways to deal with the pressure, including hiring contractors to help you with specific tasks and/or projects (we'll get to that later in the book). The first way to minimize feeling overwhelmed is with good, sound time management.

Multi-tasking

I'm a big multi-tasker. I usually have about twenty tabs open in my Internet browser. I like to knit and watch TV at the same time. But when I'm working, I absolutely *don't* believe in multi-tasking.

Study after study has shown that when you multi-task, you won't do any of the tasks well. Because you've divided your attention among different things, you simply can't attend to any one of them with the care and quality that they require.

I'm not talking about things like doing the laundry while you're working. I tossed in a load of whites right before I sat down to write this chapter.

But you won't find me going back to put those clothes in the dryer (or even thinking about them, usually) until I'm done with this particular work period.

The kind of multi-tasking I'm talking about includes things like checking e-mail while you're writing a report or popping into social media while you're on the phone with a client.

If you're trying to do two or three or more tasks at a time, you just aren't giving the attention any one task requires to anything you're doing. At best, you're doing an average job at all of them.

I know a lot of people who say they love multi-tasking and who say they're really good at it. Research indicates otherwise, and the results I've seen from most of these people support the research.

Unplugging

Often, even if you're great at managing your time, other people who are unused to the entrepreneurial lifestyle believe that if you're not working a traditional nine-to-five job, you're available 24/7.

Plus, our culture has developed into a place where you have to be available all the time. Years ago, people would call you at home, and if you didn't answer, they'd call back another time. If they couldn't reach you for a couple of weeks, they'd send you a letter.

Then answering machines came into the picture, allowing people to leave messages for you so that you could call them back when you got home. Then mobile phones made it possible for people to reach you wherever you are, whether you're in a movie, driving the car, in the bathroom, or on a completely different continent.

The problem for entrepreneurs is that we need "unplugged time" to create and develop ideas. How much can you realistically accomplish when your phone is ringing or beeping when you get texts or e-mails, or when your laptop is chiming with every incoming e-mail?

When you stop working to answer the phone, send a text, or write an e-mail, it takes you some time to get your brain back into the groove of what you were doing before. If you are interrupted regularly, you're severely impacting your productivity.

These days it's critical to unplug—turn off the Internet, shut down the computer (sometimes), and get away from the phone—so that you can truly focus on your ideas. This focus will allow you greater creativity and clarity. You do your best work when you can remain undisturbed for long periods of time. That's why you need to unplug!

So how do you unplug? When you're working, turn off the phone ringers—all of them. Disable alerts in your e-mail software, and make sure your mobile doesn't send you alerts for e-mails and texts. (I keep all of these alerts turned off at all times, which is why I'm probably the worst person to send a text message to.)

If you're really brave, just tell people that you're unplugging during a specific time period every day. But don't expect that to be easy. Friends and family members often call when it's convenient for them, even if it's during your working hours.

My sister, who's a dentist with a long commute, calls me when she's driving home from work. If I'm working though, I won't answer the phone because the ringers are turned off (sorry, Anne!). But because my relationship with my sister is a priority for me, I try to plan for times when I know she's driving home from work, so that I can take the time out to talk with her and enjoy the conversation without feeling pulled back to whatever I was working on when the phone rang.

In addition to those folks who don't understand what you do, you may discover that friends who do, in fact, "get it" may have a different concept of work ethic than you do. You may discover that other entrepreneurs make time for long lunches and phone calls that you can't or won't break away for. It's important to set boundaries with *everyone,* whether they understand it or not. If you don't give yourself uninterrupted time that you need to build your business, then you'll never have the focus you need.

Mindfulness

Mindfulness is about putting all of your focus on the one thing you're doing right now. For example, if you're buttering your toast, just *butter your toast.* Don't talk to someone while you're doing it. Don't listen to the news or watch TV. Don't do what I used to do and try to read while you're buttering that toast (that was particularly difficult). Just *butter the toast.* Pay attention to it. Think about how much butter you really need. Think about how close to the edges you can get. Really focus on what you're doing in the moment.

You might be wondering why I'm talking about buttering your toast in a book on business. Mindfulness takes practice, and it happens to be easiest to practice on boring, silly moments, like buttering your toast.

The first time I did the exercise of focusing on buttering my toast, I stood in my kitchen thinking, "This is quite possibly the dumbest exercise I've ever made myself do." Later I noticed that my toast was buttered perfectly. It was the tastiest toast I had ever eaten. Being mindful and focusing on the moment gives you the opportunity to do things exceptionally well.

There are loads of mindfulness exercises. I found the toast one and others in the book, *How to Train A Wild Elephant* by Jan Chosen Bays. Some other exercises she mentions are making sure you don't leave a trace of yourself all day long and spending the day doing everything with your opposite hand.

While they might seem silly, these exercises (and others) are quite helpful in terms of becoming more mindful of virtually every aspect of your life. You become more aware of how you show up in the world, and you become more aware of how you spend your time. Spend a few days with mindfulness exercises, and you'll become more thoughtful in the way you work so that you can do *better* work and be more productive.

Relationships

Relationships can have a *huge* impact on your ability to succeed. Without the encouragement of my husband, there's no way I'd be where I am today. It's his steadfast support and belief in me that keeps me going when I start to doubt myself.

When I told my husband I wanted to break a Guinness World Record, he didn't look at me like I was crazy. He said, "Go for it!"

And when I told him that the way it had to be done would cost over $20,000 and that I planned to find sponsors to help me with the event, he said, "Go for it!"

I can't even begin to tell you what that's worth. If you have or can find that kind of support in your friends or family members, you have a huge advantage over everyone else.

If you don't have support from your friends or family members, I encourage you to find other entrepreneurs who can be supportive. You'll need a village to keep you on track and mindful of what you're working toward (more on that later).

Take stock of any toxic relationships and where they fit into your overall goals. Toxic relationships, arguments, and emotionally draining people easily can detract from you making real progress in your business.

Having said that, it's very important to me that you understand that I am not necessarily saying that you should cut people out of your life. While there may be some relationships that you do choose to end because of their destructive influence in your life, there are often ways to change the relationships you have to limit their damaging potential. If, for example, your marriage isn't working or isn't creating a supportive environment for you to start and/or grow your business, take a good, hard look at *why* things aren't working, and then take action to make things better.

YOUR WORK ETHIC

In 2007, Timothy Ferriss launched a book, *The 4-Hour Work Week: Escape 9-5, Live Anywhere, and Join the New Rich,* that changed the way many entrepreneurs thought about their businesses.

In his book, Ferriss talked about ways to structure your business so that you have employees and staff members who manage the day-to-day operations, while you manage from afar, checking in on your business at certain times and limiting your involvement to a mere four hours every week.

It's an amazing concept, and for those who had never heard of doing business in this way, it was transformative. For those of us who had been outsourcing for years, it was encouraging. However, as much as I enjoyed the book and the strategies Tim outlined, I realized three things.

First, seventy-five percent of small businesses have no employees. Most small businesses have a hard time making ends meet, much less finding the resources to hire employees so that the business owner can vacation on the Riviera or take pottery lessons in Crete (or whatever, you get my point). So for many entrepreneurs who spend well over a regular forty-hour work week making their businesses run, the idea of a four-hour work week might be a difficult concept to even consider.

Second, most successful small businesses need the contributions of an invested owner, someone who cares deeply about the success or failure of the company. Talk to any company that offers franchises about what they've discovered is the single ingredient that determines whether their franchise owners will be a success or a failure, and they'll tell you immediately that that ingredient is the involvement of the business owner.

As a business owner, you can't show that you care deeply about your business if you're only there four hours a week. In small businesses, especially those where there is interaction with the owner, if you're not there, your employees are likely to become less committed and less invested in their jobs and in contributing to the success of the company.

In the early days of my career, I consulted with magazine publishing companies to help them take their printed content from magazines and turn it into digital content they could sell online. One of these magazine publishing companies was a small business with fewer than one hundred employees, and pretty much every employee had, at one time or another, met the owner.

He'd come in, walk around, ask an employee what he or she was doing, have a meeting or two with his vice president and some managers, and then he'd leave, flying out to St. Barts or someplace. Every so often, he'd lead a meeting to tell the employees what was going on in the company, and inevitably, he'd talk about his new boat or a new vacation home.

Following encounters with the owner of the company, employees often wondered why they were working so hard when their leader barely did a thing. The perception of the employees was that they were working tirelessly to make the company a success so that the owner could go lie on a beach somewhere. And while yes, that's their job, and yes, they're getting paid to work, the message that your employees are minions who work so that you don't have to work is *not* the message you want to send to your employees.

Third, I knew that those of us who work with entrepreneurs were going to face a challenge in terms of *sweat equity,* or the time and energy that our clients were willing to put into the beginnings of their companies.

The concept of a four-hour work week is not necessarily appropriate for startups, unless you're a startup with money to burn. Most startups begin with the investment of the sweat equity of the owner. That's when *you* work hard and put in the time, the energy, and the hours to grow your business to success. As your business grows, you take on employees or outsource to contractors when there are too many tasks for you to handle or when you can afford to delegate the work that you're not the best at or that you don't enjoy. But it's not something that most businesses do from the start.

If you are in a business that's in growth, then implementing the ideas from Tim's book can make your company run more efficiently and make your life more enjoyable. But always remember that businesses run better when the person who cares the most about the success or failure of the company is present and participatory.

In a more general sense, remember that your work ethic does matter. Good, sound business requires diligence, determination, perseverance, dedication, and patience.

YOUR MONEY MINDSET

Your money mindset is the way you're programmed to think about money—what you're capable of earning, what your skills and talents are worth, how you spend money, how you invest it, how you fear having it and losing it.

We're all programmed from the start to think about money in a certain way. If you grew up without money, it can be difficult to envision yourself as a prosperous person. But it goes beyond just whether you had money or didn't when you were growing up. Your money mindset is determined by how your parents thought about money and how they spent it, plus the experiences you've had as an adult.

For example, I grew up comfortably. I don't remember anyone ever worrying about not being able to put food on the table, and my sister and I went to good schools and always had nice clothes to wear. But my impression looking back is that we lived a little outside our means. I know that my parents invested and did *some* financial planning, but I remember my mom sitting at the dining room table writing out bills and paying credit card bills and fretting about family finances.

I also know that my grandparents were deeply affected by the Great Depression, my grandmother in particular, and as a result, always scrimped and saved every penny for the rest of their lives. I'm pretty sure that my grandparents' fears and worries had a big impact on my mom and her ideas about money, and ultimately, affected me and my ideas about money, too.

So while my family was indeed comfortable and our basic needs were more than met, I also grew up with a strong fear of money and never having enough of it. As a result, when I went through my own financial struggles during a rough patch in the early years of my business, I experienced anxiety attacks and found myself obsessed with trying to find a way out of the problems.

Over the years, I've had many clients who have had all kinds of brain junk attached to their money mindsets. I've worked with clients who were reluctant to invest in their businesses, clients who didn't know how to manage their finances, and clients who were raised with the idea that they could only reach a certain financial level and couldn't surpass that.

Whatever your money mindset is, it will have a huge impact on your level of success. If you're operating out of a place of fear or lack, you'll make decisions that are based in fear and lack. Decisions made from this mindset are almost always bad decisions because they're almost always short-term decisions made to avoid something (usually the pain of fear or anxiety) in the immediate without regard for the long-term consequences.

When you make decisions from a place of strength and courage, your decisions are made with a calm mind and a peaceful heart. You can think more clearly, and you can take into account both the short-term and long-term benefits and consequences with a wider perspective.

So how do you get from having a "lack mindset" to having an "abundance mindset?" I'm going to give it to you straight: It isn't easy.

The first step is to determine where the lack mindset comes from. Are you *really* short on money, or do you just fear being without it?

If you really are short on money, take a good, hard, honest look at your financial situation. Many of my clients have found that simple, smart budgeting has made a world of difference between feeling lack and feeling abundance. There are some wonderful resources for learning how to assess your financial situation and start a budget on the web site for this book (http://BusinessInBlueJeans.com/book).

Sometimes budgeting isn't enough to address your financial concerns because your sense of lack really does come from not having enough money to cover all of your expenses, even with a really good budget, even if you cut your expenses to the bare bones. In that case, it might be time to consider a job that can cover your expenses while you're starting and growing your business.

That's hard for a lot of people to hear, but some of my most successful clients took part-time jobs to make ends meet while they got their businesses up and running.

When you're in a part-time job that you don't really want because you're trying to make your entrepreneurial dreams come true, there are three things that can keep you going:

1. The knowledge that this job is giving you the resources you need to make what you *really* want possible.

2. The gratitude that you have a job that does provide the resources you need to make your dreams come true.

3. The realization that this is what you *don't* want.

Let me explain that third point a little bit. One of my clients works in a job that she despises. But by the time this book is published, however, she won't be working at that company anymore, and the reason for that is that being faced every day with something she doesn't want is as powerful as going home each evening to the thing she really *does* want.

Sometimes the thing you don't want is as powerful a motivator as the thing you do want.

That's why not having enough money can sometimes be an extraordinary motivator to keep you on track and working to achieve your goals. When you have enough money to keep you satisfied, sometimes it's easy to let a day or two pass without making progress in your business plan, because there's nothing prodding you ahead.

However, if you're going to take a job while you're building your business, make sure that you get really clear on your *fire* so that you know exactly what you're working toward so that you can think of it every day that you get up and go to that job.

Speaking of fire…

THE FIRE

THE FIRE

I f you want to get your business going, if you *really* want to make your business a success, the first thing you need is *fire*.

It might be a spark, or it might be one of those fantastic fires in the fireplace in the middle of winter, the one that keeps you warm. What you don't want, though, is an uncontrolled forest fire. You want a controlled, sustained burn that keeps your business going for the long haul.

WHY FIRE MATTERS

Did you ever wonder why there are so many self-help and motivational books out there? Ever wonder why motivational speakers are so popular and inspirational quotes proliferate in social media?

It's because many people have lost sight of the fire. It's because so many people are living without the slightest clue about what really matters to them.

The fire is what provides the motivation. It's what gets you out of bed in the morning. It's what gets you working late at night. It's what keeps you moving forward and making progress, no matter what stands in your way.

When you have that fire in your belly and when it's properly channeled, you don't need motivational books or inspirational quotes to spur you to action. The *fire itself* provides all of that *for* you.

TWO SOURCES OF THE FIRE

There are two sources of the fire in your belly. The first source is what I call the *heart,* the reason why you do what you do. The second is what I call the *glow,* the thing you love doing. Each provides a different source of motivation and energy toward your business success.

Why You Need Both the Heart and the Glow

Without the heart, you lack a fundamental reason for *why* you're doing what you're doing. And without the fundamental *why*, you lose sight of the bigger picture. The heart provides the foundation for all that you do.

> **The fire provides all the motivation you need to spur you to action.**

Without the glow, you lack the day-to-day joy in the business. Without the glow, you lose sight of *enjoying* your business.

You need both the heart and glow to create the fire of your business—the motivation and the inspiration to keep moving forward in the face of any and all challenges.

The Heart

In an actual flame, the vapors at the center don't die off because oxygen can't get into that part. That's what I refer to as the *heart* in your fire. It's the stuff at the center of your flame, the core of your very being, the source of all of your inspiration and motivation.

The heart is what your business makes possible—in your life, in your community, in the world. It's the thing you're really fighting for.

For me, the heart is my family. Spending high-quality time with my husband and having as much time with our extended families as we can get is vitally important to me. My own family lives nearby, so that means we have weekly dinners with my dad and stepmom and regular, rowdy family breakfasts with my sister's family, which includes the most amazing niece and nephew one could ever have. But Leo's family is spread out quite a bit, which means quite a bit of travel to see his family in South America and Europe.

At the heart of my flame are the things that are most important to me: having quality, relaxed time with Leo on a daily basis and having the time and funds available to spend time with each and every member of our families throughout the year.

The heart of my flame also encompasses being able to give back to my community and to the causes that are important to me. It's important to me to do good in the world.

Remember when I talked about your Why Dollars in the last section of this book? Those Why Dollars are the financial embodiment of the *heart*. When I planned out my Why Dollars, I factored in how much I wanted to spend on travel to see our family members around the globe. I also included amounts that I wanted to donate to charity and my pet causes each month. These numbers helped me to get a clear, quantified, tangible sense of where my business needed to go.

The heart of your flame is what lies at the core of your being, the thing that your business makes possible. Maybe the heart of your flame is a cause, your church, a feeling of safety and security, or maybe the heart of your flame is family, just like mine is. Whatever it is, you have to know it and feel it, deep in your belly.

Discovering the Heart

Maybe you're not sure what the heart of your business is. Maybe you haven't ever thought about it. Now is the time to ask the hard questions and to do some soul-searching to discover it.

The heart keeps you working when you're tired, when you're frustrated, when you're doing boring paperwork. It's what keeps you going when your latest marketing campaign doesn't yield the results you wanted. It keeps you motivated when you haven't yet achieved the level of success that you hoped for. It's the key to everything.

To discover the heart, you have to get clear on what your values are. What matters most to you?

HOMEWORK ASSIGNMENT:
DISCOVERING THE HEART

Newbie:

Make a list of values that matter to you; then circle the five to ten values that matter most. Of the values you've identified as most important, which ones do you want to see embodied in your business?

Then write down your answers to these questions:

1. What are the things you want to accomplish, not just in business, but in life?

2. When you're old and gray, what do you want to be able to tell your grandchildren that you did?

Existing Business Owner:

If you're already in business, this exercise can apply to you, too.

1. Does your business embody the values that are important to you?

2 Do you struggle with staying motivated? (If so, definitely go to the "Newbies" section and do the entire exercise!)

The Glow

The glow is the second part of the fire. This is the part of the fire that the world sees. Where the heart is what your business makes possible, the glow is *what your business is about.*

My business is about showing aspiring, budding, and growing entrepreneurs that the American Dream is alive and achievable. It's about guiding small business owners to incorporate the fundamentals that have stood the test of time into their businesses and to fuse them with new ways of thinking that breed unparalleled success.

The glow, for me, comes from a deep belief in this philosophy and in loving what I do more than anything else I've ever done or than anything else I can imagine doing.

I love working one-on-one with my clients. I love seeing them making progress. I love seeing them get excited when they see the light at the end of the tunnel and when they start to get results that have eluded them before. I love working with my corporate clients, giving them great ideas, and watching their large audiences get recharged when their favorite brands evolve.

I love writing and I love speaking. I was born to be a teacher. And because of how much I love doing these things, I wake up every single day excited about what I get to do, excited that I get paid to do it.

So what's the glow for you? What's the thing that *you* love doing more than anything else?

Discovering the Glow

On occasion, I work with a client who contacts me because she knows she wants to start a business, but she just isn't sure what kind of business she wants to start. Often, the process of helping this kind of client to create a business requires discovering the glow.

There are two ways to discover the glow. You can start by looking back at your life and looking for the constants. In fact, this is how I discovered my calling in life. When I looked back over my entire life, I realized that writing, speaking, and teaching have always been a part of who I am.

The second way to discover the glow is to think about your ideal week. If you were given a week to spend however you wanted (relating to your business, of course), without any concern for funding, what would you do? How would you spend your time? Would you spend a lot of time with other people? How much, how far, and how often would you travel? Would you speak in front of groups, travel to oversee factories, have meetings to make sales? Open your mind to the possibilities and map out the days and what you'd be doing.

HOMEWORK ASSIGNMENT:
DISCOVERING THE GLOW

Newbie:

Answer the following:

1. What things have been constant throughout your life?

2. What things do you love doing most?

3. Describe your ideal week. What does that look like?

Other example questions to ponder:

- Do you like to work with people, or is your work solitary?

- Do you work from home or in an office?

- How much do you travel?

- What percentage of your business do you want to be passive vs. active income?

- How much of your business do you want to do online?

Existing Business Owner:

Answer the following:

1. Do you get to do the things that you love most in your business as it currently exists?

2. Do you do a lot of things you don't love?

3. Describe your ideal week. What does that look like? How closely does your current business resemble that description?

A NOTE ON PURPOSE

If you've spent any time around the personal growth movement or, say, Oprah, you may have heard a lot about "passion" and "life purpose." It seems like most coaches talk about passion or purpose or finding your life's path these days.

Do you need to find your purpose in life? Not necessarily. For some, it's a lifelong journey. For others, purpose or calling is a thing they discover early on.

My husband, Leo, is a professional drummer. Originally from Uruguay, Leo knew at age thirteen that he wanted to be a musician, from the first moments that he heard Jimi Hendrix. He started looking for similar music, found Led Zeppelin, and finally made his way around to Frank Zappa. The humor and the rhythm in Zappa's music resonated so deeply with Leo that he knew for sure that he was meant to be a drummer.

At the time, Leo's family couldn't buy him a drum kit, so he played around on a friend's kit whenever he could. By his late teens, he was still so certain that he was meant to be a musician that he got a job just so he could buy a drum kit. He finally started studying officially at age nineteen, a full six years after he first discovered his fire.

By the time Leo was twenty-five, he was part of not one, but *three* of the most significant bands in the history of Uruguay. By the time he was twenty-nine, one of those bands had earned the first gold and platinum records for rock albums in the entire history of the country and eventually had a *stack* of them to their name.

To this day, Leo is referred to as the "mythical" drummer of the 1980s and is a sought-after musician in Uruguay. Former band members from groups he played with in Spain and in the Canary Islands want to know when he's coming back to town so they can jam. Journalists in Uruguay have even gone so far as to locate him in the United States to interview him.

I tell you this not to brag, although I *am* super proud of Leo's accomplishments. The reason I'm sharing Leo's story is because he's an *amazing* example of someone who understands what's in his soul—in his case, rhythm.

I once asked Leo, "How did you know for sure that's what you were supposed to do?" Leo says he just *knew*.

There are people who just seem to know their calling, practically from birth. If you're one of those people, congratulations and more power to you!

But what if you haven't discovered your true calling in life? Does that mean that you're somehow lacking or that you can't have the kind of success that Leo has had? *No!* Absolutely not!

Actually, my guess is that if you're feeling like you haven't discovered your calling, your purpose, or your mission in life, it's really just that you haven't found your fire, and it's probably because that fire's either burning low or temporarily extinguished. So let's take a look at some of the challenges to fire, what I call "the Extinguishers."

THE EXTINGUISHERS

The Kitchen Sink

When I was a little girl, I wanted to do *everything.* I wanted to be a teacher, a writer, a fashion designer, a violinist. I wanted to be a mom, a wife, a psychologist, and a scientist. But nothing really called out to me so much that I was willing to eschew everything else in favor of it.

Over the course of my lifetime, there have been many, many things that have interested me. I've had an abundance of business ideas, career opportunities, and possible paths that excited me. Sometimes the Kitchen Sink stems from a person having a lot of interests and not knowing which one to pursue.

HOMEWORK ASSIGNMENT:
CLEANING OUT THE SINK

Newbies:

What really resonates with you? What makes your heart sing? What brings you the most joy? What things have been constants throughout your life?

If you have a plethora of interests, it may simply mean that you love having variety in your life, which means you may need to create a business where each day is a little different.

In addition for looking for the constants and the things that bring you joy, also look for signals that tell you the characteristics you want to incorporate into your business.

Sometimes, though, the Kitchen Sink comes from a person not knowing how to grow one business, and thinking that having "everything but the kitchen sink" will bring in more business.

For example, I have a client who is a virtual assistant. When I looked at her web site during our initial business analysis, I discovered a bunch of promotions related to a network marketing cosmetics business. When I asked her what the cosmetics stuff had to do with her virtual assisting business, she said that she'd signed up for the cosmetics business because she wasn't making enough money with her virtual assisting and wanted to supplement her income with another business.

She didn't realize that by adding another business to her lineup, especially one that was so out of sync with her existing business, she was creating a Kitchen Sink effect and confusing her potential clients so much that they simply didn't hire her at all.

Once we pulled the out-of-sync product line and started to clarify her brand, she got a lot clearer about what actions to take to grow her virtual assisting business and her potential clients were no longer confused.

Over the years, I've seen *many* people bring in the Kitchen Sink to cover their bases, and the story is always the same. It's never a successful strategy, and it never makes sense to me.

If you can't grow one business, why add another business that you have to grow? That makes no sense!

Instead of making things harder on yourself, hone in on the one thing that you really want to do and focus on building *just* that business.

HOMEWORK ASSIGNMENT:
CLEANING OUT THE SINK

Existing Business Owners:

Examine your business. Have you added product lines or extra services that don't make sense with your business in order to boost

> revenue? Which products or services can you eliminate to clarify your brand?

No Fire

Maybe you feel as if you have *no* fire. There's no heart, no glow, nothing that really excites you. What happens *then?*

Everybody's different. You don't have to jump up and down to show your passion. You might be more low-key or laid back about things. Look for what fire means *to you.*

Maybe you haven't found your "thing" yet. If that's the case, experiment with your options. Read about different careers and industries. Look for anything that interests you. Spend a day in your local library or noodling around on About.com and see if anything sparks your interest.

Or, maybe there's something else going on. If you know that you're generally a person who gets excited about things, but you haven't been excited about anything in a while, or if you just can't muster enthusiasm for anything at all, you might be depressed. If that's the case, please find some help so you can get your fire back!

Uncertainty

Sometimes not knowing what your purpose is stems from not giving yourself permission to pursue your dreams.

Maybe you've been taught that dreaming is a bad thing. Or maybe you learned there's a certain way to live your life—grow up, go to school, get a job, get married, have kids, work, work, work, retire, join a bridge club.... Maybe you learned that deviating from that path is a bad thing, and you're only just starting to ask yourself if there's more to life.

Maybe you didn't know that it's okay to *love* the thing that you get paid to do. Maybe you didn't know that you can get paid to do the thing you love. (Those actually *are* two different sentences.)

Uncertainty comes when you haven't given yourself permission to pursue the dream of owning your own business and growing it into a successful enterprise.

If this is your challenge, why haven't you given yourself permission yet? Are you ready to do it now?

Grandiosity

I've always had big ideas. Big, *big* ideas. But pursuing them hasn't always been easy. There was a time when I found ways to sabotage big ideas almost as quickly as I came up with them. Whenever I had a big idea, I'd envision what it would be like if that idea became reality, and I'd find all kinds of roadblocks. Promptly, I'd dismiss the idea.

It wasn't until I realized this pattern of thinking was holding me back from being able to do all kinds of fantastic things that I decided to rid myself of this damaging brain junk so I could start realizing my big ideas. As soon as I did that, I was on my way to breaking the Guinness World Records® record for the world's longest uninterrupted live webcast.

When I decided I wanted to hold a Guinness World Records® title, I really didn't know what kind of record I could break. I'm not super old or super short or super tall. I'm not an athlete or a competitive eater. But I *am* knowledgeable about technology, and I can talk a *lot*. So my first goal was to find a record that I *could* break.

Believe me, I could've sabotaged the entire project before it got started. But when you have a big idea, it gets a lot less scary if you work backward from the goal to create a workable plan. So once I figured out which record I wanted to break and had gotten approval from Guinness World Records® to make my attempt, I started working backward, breaking each step down until every step was manageable and reasonable.

I worked backward for each goal of this event, from finish to start. For example, when I discovered that the event was going to cost me upwards of $20,000, I realized I would need sponsors to help me fund the event. But I didn't make finding sponsors my goal. I made "research companies that might be interested in partnering in this kind of event" my goal. Some days, my goal for the day was to compose an e-mail. Some days my goal was to contact a certain number of companies or possible guests for the event.

It was this strategy that allowed me to plan a thirty-six hour event with both online and in-person components, thirty-three speakers, seven witnesses, with full sponsorship inside of just fifty-five days. That's right, fifty-five days.

Big ideas *are* possible, and you must learn to set aside your fears, anxieties, and doubts and give yourself permission to dream big. You just have to stop holding yourself back and fearing your own greatness.

Our greatness is terrifying because when most people envision embodying their full potential, what they envision is akin to being on a very tall, very narrow pillar, something that's highly unstable. We don't fear being amazing because being amazing will be scary. We fear being amazing because we're afraid we can't *keep* being amazing and we'll fall from a great height, which we perceive as infinitely more painful than a fall from being average.

If there's one thing that I can promise you, it's that a lifetime of average, with the ache of never having achieved your true potential for greatness, is much, much more painful than failure could ever be. It's certainly more boring.

I know several people who have failed big. My friend and mentor Larry Winget, who had his own show, *Big Spender,* on A&E, has written in his books about being a millionaire, then declaring bankruptcy and pulling himself back up by his bootstraps. Jack Canfield has talked in interviews about how he was a millionaire and lost it all, then found success again. Donald Trump has failed at several things, but he doesn't live in shame. He gets up, dusts himself off, and tries something bigger and better next time.

> **If there's one thing that I can promise you, it's that the ache of never having achieved your true potential for greatness, is much, much more painful than failure could ever be.**

In fact, these mentors inspired me to pull myself back up when I once felt like a huge failure. And I went on to great success, including breaking that record. There's no shame in failing. There's only shame in not letting yourself try because you're afraid.

Now, sometimes it's not *you* who's holding you back. Sometimes a challenge to your grandiosity comes from other people.

Sometimes when you have a big goal, other people can become naysayers that discourage you from taking action. It's not that they're mean or evil. Most of the time they want to help you, but they're afraid of you trying something big, but failing and getting hurt. They may not understand what you're trying to do *at all*. And sometimes, you'll encounter people who are quite simply envious of your guts, determination, and ability to see the world in a different way.

With people who just don't get what you're trying to do, sometimes it's best to wait until after you've accomplished your goals (or at least are on your way) to tell them about it. That way they can celebrate your success instead of trying to protect you or pull you down.

Don't let your fears about being too grandiose get in the way of your fire. Give yourself permission to dream *big*.

Time

Another challenge you may face is that sometimes it feels like there just isn't enough time in the day, no matter how hard you try to stay focused and efficient with your time management. Sometimes you simply wish there were more hours in the day.

Time is a particular challenge for entrepreneurs who are starting or growing a business while holding down a job. If you work a full day and come home to work on your business at night, you'll be tired and you won't feel like doing much…right?

Wrong! Remember your fire? That's what provides the energy to continue making strides when you're tired or only have a little time. In fact, if you've discovered your true fire, then when you're at work thinking about going home to work on your business, you'll feel lighter and happier and more energetic.

Over the years, I've had clients who had all kinds of struggles. I've had clients who worked full-time jobs, had families, and had little time for entrepreneurship. I've had clients who were caregivers and only had a few *minutes each day* to devote to their businesses. But because each of them was driven by the fire, they were eager to keep making progress. That said, if you want more time, there *are* ways to create it.

Smart Time Management Strategies

Even with fire moving you forward, if time is a challenge for you, you'll want to implement time management strategies to help you make the most of the time you do have to work on your business.

Keep a Time Journal

This is a strategy I learned from another friend and mentor, John Morgan, bestselling author of *Brand Against the Machine*. For two days, keep a journal of exactly how you spend your time. Set a timer to go off every fifteen minutes. When it goes off, write down exactly what you were doing.

The act of tracking your time makes you more aware of how you're spending it. This allows you to get clearer about how you want to spend your time and to start scheduling things so you can be more effective.

Specific Focus

Keeping the time journal also shows you how many times you pull yourself away from a task to check e-mail or social media. When you're working on a project, keep specific focus on that project. Don't allow yourself to get distracted by anything else. You'll be more effective and complete tasks faster, because you won't waste the time it takes to get your attention back onto your task when you've been sidetracked.

Turn off the ringer on your phone. Turn off e-mail and social media notifications. Turn off *anything* that has the potential to distract you from what that you're working on.

Making Others Aware

When I'm going to work on a project, I let people know what I'm doing. For example, right before I sat down to write this chapter, I told my husband, "I'll be writing a chapter in my book." Since we've talked about the focus I need for this project, letting him know that I was working on something that required my full attention meant he wouldn't interrupt me unless there was an emergency. This strategy can work with kids, too. Find ways to make it fun, like coming up with silly codes for announcing when you're working and when you're done.

We live in a world where most people seem to expect immediate responses to their texts, e-mails, and phone calls. You'll want to make it clear to friends and family members that when you're working, you may not always answer your phone. Let people know that you've changed the settings on your computer and phone so you're not notified by distracting sounds when you receive e-mails or text messages. By clearly communicating with the people in your life, you guide expectations—they don't guide you.

The Ember Challenge

The Ember Challenge is a test of your fire like no other. When you've tried to turn your fire into a business and your attempt has failed (or seems like it has), the fire in your belly wanes, dying down to its last, barely glowing embers.

Entrepreneurs in this situation are likely burned out, frustrated, and tired; they've spent tens of thousands of dollars on seminars, workshops, masterminds, coaching, digital products, marketing schemes...and nothing has worked. (We'll get to *that* issue later in the book.)

When you've tried to grow your business for a long, long time and haven't seen a return, when your business isn't thriving, there's no fuel to keep the fire going. And that's when the fire starts to die out.

Have you ever seen a fire that's dying? There's nothing sadder, if you've seen the glory of the flames before the fire is allowed to die out. But there's a secret that a lot of people don't know. I only know this because my husband, being from a country where the love of fire-grilled meat is practically a cultural requirement, has taught me a lot about fire.

> **If you feel like you've lost your fire, remember that it's not gone. You just have to stoke the fire to get the flames going again.**

In Uruguay, they grill in a very specific way. It's called *asado,* and it consists of burning wood and cooking food (mostly meat) on a grill that sits over the embers of the fire. I don't actually eat meat (most of the time). But when I'm in Uruguay, I don't even bother to resist, especially if we visit the Mercado del Puerto, where there are about ten different asado restaurants. But in talking to the *asadors* who cook the meat over the embers, what I learned is that the embers are the *best* heat for grilling because they're hot, but not *too* hot. They're the perfect temperature.

You see, embers are the product of a dying fire, but they're still burning hot. And if you feel like you've lost your fire, remember that it's not gone. It's not lost. You just have to stoke the fire and give it some fuel to get the flames going again.

Stoking the Fire

To get that fire going again, you need to give the fire some fuel. Sometimes a little success is enough to fuel the fire. Sometimes you need more.

I once experienced the Ember Challenge myself, and I discovered that hiring a business coach and mentor who could take a look at my business and tell me what I was missing helped me enormously. Suddenly, I had a clear path, things I could tweak in my business, and I was getting results! That was a huge boost and stoked the embers back into a full flame.

The trick of stoking the fire is to determine why your flames went out in the first place. What caused your fire to die down? Was it discouragement? Was it boredom? Determine the cause and you'll most likely find a solution.

THE FIRE, PROPERLY CHANNELED

The thing about the fire is that it does need to be channeled properly. When I say that, I mean that the fire in your belly isn't enough to create success. Getting clarity on what you want most in life (the heart) and loving what you do (the glow) isn't enough to create a successful business. You need more.

Let's take a look at the next thing on the list: expertise.

EXPERTISE

EXPERTISE

etting your brain junk sorted out and having fire in your belly are important, but they're almost irrelevant without expertise.

WHAT IS EXPERTISE?

Expertise is, in short, mastery over something. It's when you're really, really good at something.

Apple has mastered the art of creating cutting-edge, groundbreaking products that have changed the way we look at media. Zappos has covered the art of unparalleled service. I have expertise in guiding small business owners and entrepreneurs to realize the full potential in themselves and in their businesses. Having expertise is knowing more about a topic and doing something better than most people.

WHY DOES EXPERTISE MATTER?

Expertise matters for two reasons. First, expertise is half of the equation for a successful business.

Audiophiles (people who are enthusiastic and knowledgeable about sound quality and reproduction in sound reproduction) use a term to describe the specific place where you should stand between the speakers to hear a recording *precisely* as it was intended to be heard. That place is called the "sweet spot." Stand between two speakers in the exact right spot and you'll hear every note and every nuance, whether you're listening to Jimi Hendrix demolish a guitar riff or Isaac Stern play Paganini.

In your business, there's a sweet spot as well. Your sweet spot is the place between your fire and your expertise, where the two overlap. In fact, if you drew a Venn diagram and put fire and expertise in the diagram, the place where the circles overlap should be the heart and soul of your business (see below).

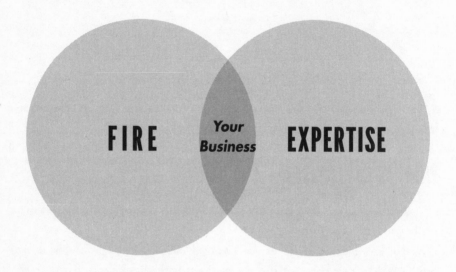

If you take what you love doing and merge it with what you do well, that's what your business should be about. That business will have the highest likelihood of success, because the fire in your belly will keep you motivated, and your expertise will ensure that you do what you do *really* well, which is a large part of why people will come back to you again and again.

The second reason that expertise is important is centered on *authenticity* and *integrity*, which I believe are critically important to doing good business.

In my time, I've come across an awful lot of "gurus" who say that you don't have to actually *be* an expert to position yourself as an expert. What they're not telling you, however, is that if you position yourself as an expert without having the "chops" to back it up, you'll feel like a fraud, and eventually you'll be found out and customers won't come back to you.

If you feel like a fraud because you have brain junk, please refer to the first chapter of this book. But if you feel like a fraud for a reason (e.g., you're promising something you can't deliver), then it's time to start making some changes.

Good business means backing up your claims with real expertise and doing your work with *consistency* and *excellence*—reliably performing at the peak of your capabilities—and delivering what you promise.

> **"Good business means backing up your claims with real expertise and delivering on what you promise."**

As my friend Larry Winget says, "Do what you say you're going to do, when you say you're going to do it." I couldn't agree more. This one simple statement is a *huge* key to success.

WHAT IF YOU DON'T HAVE EXPERTISE?

I know a few of you are thinking, "Heck, I'm not good at anything," and to that I laugh heartily and say, "What a bunch of hooey!"

We're *all* good at something, every single one of us. In fact, I've never encountered someone who wasn't good at *something*. I've encountered a lot of people who *believe* they're not good at anything, but I've always discovered that they're wrong. Sometimes it's just a matter of uncovering your hidden talents and skills. Sometimes it's a matter of realizing that certain things *are* marketable skills.

Discovering Your Expertise

Discovering your expertise is a lot like discovering the glow in your fire. It requires looking at your history.

HOMEWORK ASSIGNMENT:
DISCOVERING YOUR EXPERTISE

Newbies:

First, make a list of your areas of expertise. Include everything, even things that you might not think of as relevant to your business. Factor in anything that shows up in the Inventory of Success that you created in the Brain Junk chapter.

Then, for each area of expertise that you listed, rate each item on a scale of 1-10, with 10 being the highest level of expert status you could possibly attain.

Now, create your own Venn diagram like the one at the beginning of this chapter. What falls into both circles? What's the "sweet spot" between your Fire and your Expertise?

Now answer the following questions:

1. What could you promise to deliver consistently and reliably?

2. How will you be authentic and maintain integrity with your expertise and your promises?

Existing Business Owners:

Answer the following questions:

1. Are you operating within your level of expertise?

2. Do you only make promises that you can reliably and consistently keep?

3. Do you always do what you say you're going to do when you say you're going to do it?

4. How could you bring more integrity to your promises to your customers and clients?

5. Does your staff operate at the highest levels of their individual areas of expertise?

WHEN IT'S OKAY NOT TO HAVE EXPERTISE

There *are* times when it's okay not to be an expert. Many successful bloggers have launched their careers by allowing others a view into their learning process.

Did you see the movie *Julie and Julia*? That movie originated from a book based on a blog. A woman named Julie Powell decided to create a blog to chronicle her attempts to cook her way through Julia Child's cookbook *Mastering the Art of French Cooking*. Julie wasn't an expert in cooking when she first started out. She was, however, a writer (expertise), and, in fact, the blog she wrote was designed to garner her a book deal (fire). And since she had a true interest in learning to cook (fire), she fused all of these things into a business that became profitable.

> **You don't have to deliver massive results to have true expertise. You just have to deliver the results that you can offer with consistency and excellence.**

Lisa Lillien is another great example. Lisa was a media executive who loved food and loved to write (fire). She had no training as a nutritionist, but she had lost thirty pounds (expertise) and wanted to share how she did it with others. Since launching her blog, Hungry Girl, in 2004, she's accumulated more than a million subscribers, profitable food partnerships, and ad sales, plus she has six bestselling books and a television show that airs on the Food Network.

Note that both of these bloggers were writers to start—writing was their expertise. They took their expertise and fused it with their fire and created incredibly successful businesses. You can find examples like this all over the web.

But don't worry—this conversation isn't just limited to bloggers. There are other areas in which you don't have to have *all* the expertise in the world to be successful. I've seen personal trainers build successful careers on helping clients who just want to lose a few pounds and add exercise into their daily routine, rather than promising to help clients lose a hundred pounds. I've seen business coaches build a strong foundation for their business by helping their clients make an additional few hundred dollars a month, rather than promising to show them how to make millions.

Don't worry if you can't promise your customers or clients the world. They might not need "the world," and they might be really pleased with a bigger piece of it than they now have. You don't have to deliver *massive* results to have true expertise. You just have to deliver the results that you *can* offer with consistency and excellence.

DEVELOPING YOUR EXPERTISE

Growing your business and becoming more successful depends, in part, on developing your expertise and continuously getting better at what you do. Reading good books, taking classes and continuing education courses, and working with coaches and consultants are all excellent ways to continue to improve and expand your expertise.

You must be a constant work in progress, which, if you're really operating out of the fire in your belly, you'll probably enjoy anyway.

I read *a lot*. I've read so many books about business and entrepreneurship, personal growth, sales, networking, branding, marketing, social media, and more, I literally couldn't tell you how many books I've read. I usually have at least two or three books in progress at any time, and most of my books are dog-eared and have notes written all over them.

Another way to gain expertise is by doing something a *lot*. My friend, bestselling author David Meerman Scott, mastered being a dynamic, engaging speaker by focusing on a different part of his presentation during every speech that he gave for years. During one speech, he'd focus on where his feet were. During another speech, he'd think about the pacing of his speech.

In the book *Outliers: The Story of Success*, Malcolm Gladwell talks about the "10,000-Hour Rule," which says that you achieve mastery over something by doing that thing for 10,000 hours. So, for example, if you want to be a master violinist, you must practice diligently for about 10,000 hours (which translates to roughly ten years).

If you're not there yet, create a plan for developing your expertise so you do get there eventually. And if you are there, you should have a plan for continuing to grow and learn and keeping your knowledge up to date.

HOMEWORK ASSIGNMENTI:
DEVELOPING YOUR EXPERTISE

Newbies:

Create a plan for developing your expertise.

List classes that you can take, books that you can read, and mentors and/or coaches you can work with.

Create a timeline for these tasks.

Write down how much time each day you'll devote to developing your expertise.

Existing Business Owners:

Develop a plan for you to develop your expertise and keep your knowledge up to date.

Create a similar plan for your employees.

PACKAGING

PACKAGING

There are two parts to packaging: packaging the sweet spot between your fire and your expertise into a profitable business model, and packaging your business into a standout brand so that you can increase visibility and attract the customers that want what your business has to offer and are willing to pay for it.

In this section, I'll show you how to find out who wants what you have to offer and will pay for it, how to package your sweet spot into a viable, profitable business model, and how to create a brand that stands out in the marketplace.

This section is also what I refer to as the "workhorse section" of the business process. This is where you're going to do the grunt work. It's hard, but the payoff is huge. If you put in the sweat equity here, everything else will be a lot easier. This is where you'll lay the groundwork for everything else that will come up in subsequent chapters.

THE INTERPLAY

At this point in the process, everything turns into an interplay. Packaging is not a linear process with easy-to-define steps that you can take in order. In fact, the packaging part of creating and growing a business is a constant back-and-forth between determining what you do, who you do it for, and how you do it. There's no real "right" starting point here.

In fact, you may find that you've created a mission statement and then, when you choose your target market, you need to adjust your mission statement to better emphasize what's important to the market you want to serve.

Or you might find that you envision one kind of business structure, but as you begin to design your offerings, you realize that the model you had in mind can't quite deliver the products or services you want to offer.

> **" If you put in the sweat equity here, everything else will be a lot easier. This is where you'll lay the groundwork for everything else. "**

This is one of the reasons that books and guides to starting and growing a business can be misleading. Because you're reading this book, turning pages, I have to write in a linear order—as if these are steps you follow, in order. But in reality, you'll need to go back and forth as you move along in the packaging process.

This part of the process is fluid. As you get clear on the specifics, your business model will emerge as the best structure to deliver what your market wants in the most effective, efficient way possible.

Be prepared to go back and forth and in circles during this process. That's how it's supposed to work.

THE WEIRDNESS

This section of the book is also where you're most likely to get frustrated. I've seen it dozens of times over the years with my clients. When you're at the point where you're transforming that sweet spot between the fire and the expertise into a business, when you're creating the thing that has the potential to turn your dreams into reality, there's a lot of pressure...or at least, it feels that way.

This is where the most creativity is required. Thus, at times, you're likely to feel taxed, frustrated, and overwhelmed. *That is totally normal.*

Whether you're trying to sort out your mission statement or naming (or re-branding) your business, if you start to feel pressured, stressed out, or like you're starting to force things, sometimes you'll need to *walk away*.

Literally walk away from whatever it is that you're doing and go do something else. Stop thinking about all of it for a while.

When you step away from a mind-intensive task and allow your brain to relax, the subconscious takes over and continues to mull over the problem while you're doing something else. When it comes up with a solution, it'll pop into your conscious brain. BOOM! Sometimes it happens when you're folding laundry or when you're taking a shower or even a nap.

It may sound counterintuitive, but the truth is, sometimes forcing the creative process gets in the way of being able to do it. So during this process, if it's not coming naturally, step away and let your conscious brain rest, and *don't* feel guilty about it!

PACKAGING THE SWEET SPOT INTO A BUSINESS

Every business (and every business owner) is unique, and what one would include in a business model varies by industry. I've done my best to give you guidelines and examples that will steer you down the right path, but be aware that there are exceptions to every rule.

Getting Your Ducks in a Row

The first step in the Business in Blue Jeans process of choosing how to structure your business is to look at the results of the exercises you've done up to now. This is where you'll start putting that homework together.

The exercises you've done up to this point give you the best picture of what you want your life and your business to look like. Why does this matter in terms of creating your business model? Well, let's say, for example, in your "Discovering the Glow" exercise, you wrote that you want to work from home and you're fairly introverted, so you don't want to work with people on a daily basis. That should inform your business model: You don't want to create a business that requires you to go to an office where you deal with people every single day.

Or let's say that, when you finished your "Planning Your Whys" exercise from the Brain Junk chapter, when you started to put a dollar figure to what you want your business to make possible, you realized that to make all the things you want in life possible, your business must generate seven figures annually. In that case, you'll need a different business model than someone who's content with $50,000 a year.

It's also possible that, depending on the industry and the potential that exists in your market, you may want or need to create multiple streams of income to create a substantial annual income.

When you assemble the information you've collected about your dreams and the lifestyle you want, you'll get a good picture of the characteristics your business model should have to match up with the life you want.

This is a very different orientation to business than you'll find in most business books, but as an entrepreneur you have the luxury of being able to create your business in whatever way works best for you. This is where we really get to the heart of the Business in Blue Jeans way of doing business: in your way, in your style, *on your terms.*

Once you've collected all the information from the exercises you've done, start looking for patterns and themes.

HOMEWORK ASSIGNMENT:
GETTING YOUR DUCKS IN A ROW

Newbies:

Assemble the information from the exercises in this book.
Look for patterns and themes in your responses and list them.

Existing Business Owners:

Does your existing business work within the patterns and themes you've identified as important to you?
Can your business reach the profitability that you require for the lifestyle and dreams you identified?

Now that you have those patterns and themes assembled, you can move on to your mission statement, how your business will be structured, and what you'll offer.

Writing Your Mission Statement

There's no need to get fancy with a mission statement. A mission statement is just a statement about what you bring to the table, how you bring it, and whom you bring it to. It doesn't have to be stated in any particular way. Create a mission statement that's written in your own unique voice. For example:

- "Google's mission is to organize the world's information and make it universally accessible and useful."[1]

- Zappos' mission is "to provide the best customer service possible."[2]

- Virgin Atlantic's mission is "Safety, security and consistent delivery of the basics."[3]

- Southwest Airlines' mission is "dedication to the highest quality of customer service delivered with a sense of warmth, friendliness, individual pride, and company spirit."[4]

Your mission statement can be as short or as long as you want.

HOMEWORK ASSIGNMENT:
WRITING A MISSION STATEMENT

Looking back over the values that you identified that you wanted embodied in your business ("Discovering the Heart" exercise in The Fire chapter), for each value that you chose, what action can you take to express that value?

Example: Business in Blue Jeans

VALUE	ACTION
Independence	Teaching entrepreneurs and small business owners to create businesses that are structured to make their dream lifestyles possible

VALUE	ACTION
Prosperity	Showing entrepreneurs how to grow their businesse
Joy of being	Helping entrepreneurs to create businesses they love
Authenticity	Taking a public stance against cookie-cutter "gurus," "one-trick ponies," and get-rich-quick scam artists

Then, translate the information you've collected into a single mission statement.

Example Mission statement:

The mission of Business in Blue Jeans is to teach entrepreneurs and small business owners how to authentically create and grow businesses that they love and that are structured to make their dream lifestyles possible.

Drawing Lines in the Sand

There are times when you may want to "draw lines in the sand" and take a stance on something that is important to you or to your industry.

For example, as you can see from the sample exercise above, in my actions list, I've drawn a line in the sand with those in my industry who offer "get rich quick" schemes and who suggest that you can successfully grow a business using only one method or strategy.

Don't be afraid to stand up for what you believe in. Drawing a line in the sand can be useful in terms of narrowing your target market as well as generating publicity.

Chick-Fil-A vs. Oreos

In 2012, there were two parallel instances of drawing lines in the sand. One was overt: The COO of Chick-Fil-A, a popular fast food restaurant, made several public statements against gay marriage. It wasn't long before people were lining up on both sides of the controversy, some to boycott and some to stand in line to buy a sandwich in support.

Meanwhile, Kraft, the company that makes the Oreo cookie, posted on their Facebook wall a photo of an Oreo cookie that was made with not just one layer of white filling, but a multi-layered rainbow of fillings (for those of you who may not know, the rainbow is used in the flag representing gay pride). It wasn't a real cookie, but generated a *ton* of interest and commentary. While some said that they would never eat an Oreo cookie again, the response was overwhelmingly positive.

As of the writing of this book, the numbers aren't in yet, in terms of the results for either Oreo or Chick-Fil-A. But given our twenty-four-hour news cycle, my guess is that a lot of people will forget the controversy and just remember the brand names, benefitting both companies. That's just how it works sometimes.

> ❝ **Don't be afraid to stand up for what you believe in. Drawing a line in the sand can be useful in terms of narrowing your target market as well as generating publicity.** ❞

But it doesn't always work that way. Sometimes people remember if your company took a stance that offended them. That's why some people who are emotionally attached to the issue will remember why they do or don't support Oreo *and* Chick-Fil-A.

This is the main reason why I don't share my religious and political views in public. Unless your business is specifically related to these issues, I advise you to stay away from them, too. Why take a stance about politics and alienate half of the population? Why take a stance on religion and alienate those who don't believe the same as you?

If you run a business that's centered around politics or religion, you can take a stance in these areas, and it probably won't affect your business. For example, if you run a Christian bookstore, then you've already taken a position on religion and talking about religious issues in a blog or in marketing campaigns is fair game for you.

However, since there are plenty of other ways to draw lines in the sand besides politics and religion, you can find another way to stand out and make waves. Just make sure that you're not taking a stance just to take a stance, but rather that you're doing it authentically and that it's something you really believe in.

DrumMax

When my husband, Leo, launched DrumMax, his custom drum-building company, he discovered that many drum-building companies were using parts made in China. The parts made in China are certainly cheaper. Many custom companies use those parts because having cheaper parts meant they're able to sell their drums for a lower retail price.

Leo decided to take a difference stance with the drums his company builds. When Leo came to the United States, he followed the letter of immigration law. And while it was difficult for a period of time—he wasn't allowed to work for a period of several months, while he awaited his green card—he always felt the United States welcomed him with open arms.

Leo also believes in small businesses investing in the American economy. Plus, he's been more impressed with the quality and caliber of the parts and supplies that he's found in the States versus what he's found in other countries. So Leo drew a line in the sand, deciding that all of his drums would be labeled "Made in U.S.A."

When Leo researched using the "Made in U.S.A." label, he found out that, according to FTC rules, in order to use that label, "the product's final assembly or processing must take place in the U.S.," but the parts can, in fact, be made outside the country, depending on how far removed the manufacturing was in the process from the assembly. What that means is that you can, in some cases, take parts made outside the United States and assemble them into a product in, say, Iowa, and then say that product is "Made in the U.S.A." He also discovered that to use the "Made in U.S.A." label, "all or virtually all" of the products in a product line have to be made in the United States.

> **When you draw a line in the sand, draw a line that's authentic to you and that the people you want to sell to will find appealing.**

After learning about how weird the FTC rules were, Leo decided that, while *other* companies clearly skirt the boundaries of the rules, his stance was going to be pure. He wanted to be authentic and to have integrity with his brand. So he drew a further line in the sand: All of the components, parts, and supplies that his drums are made with are domestically created. Everything will be made in the United States of America. Period.

This particular stance can be a difficult one. It can mean that your prices will be higher across the board. And certainly, Leo's drums do cost a little more than his competitors' drums. But Leo feels that the quality is better, and the "Made in U.S.A." stance is important to him, to the quality of the drums, and to the brand. So that's the line he's drawn.

In addition to drawing in additional drummers who like the "Made in U.S.A." stance, the fact that Leo has taken a stance on *quality* makes his brand more appealing to his target market, which happens to be serious, dedicated drummers who care deeply about quality of sound.

When you draw a line in the sand, draw a line that's authentic to you *and* that the people you want to sell to will find appealing.

Be Prepared

When you take a stance, be prepared for people who won't agree with you. Sometimes taking a stance can make enemies out of those who disagree, which can be difficult to take. Make sure you're prepared and ready for people to disagree with you.

At the same time, if you're drawing a line in the sand about something you really believe in, *and it makes sense to your brand,* then it can be extremely useful.

FCUK vs. United Colors of Benetton

Companies like French Connection UK (also known as FCUK, you can see that they're starting the controversy with their very name) and United Colors of Benetton have been known for being controversial in their advertising and brand-building for years. Fashion can be a cutting-edge industry, where almost anything goes, but these two companies have a different take on why the controversy exists.

French Connection UK seems to have created a brand solely for the purpose of stirring up pointless controversy to get noticed, while for decades,

Benetton has been both praised and vilified for taking clear, strong stances on human rights, HIV, civil liberties, and other social issues. In fact, in 2000, Benetton was listed in Guinness World Records® as having had the "Most Controversial Campaign."

Creating controversy, whether for controversy's sake or to make a difference, can be successful, but if it doesn't make sense to your brand or you're not in an industry that tolerates controversy well, then I don't advise it.

HOMEWORK ASSIGNMENT:
DRAWING A LINE IN THE SAND

Newbies:

Are you interested in taking a stance?

Does it make sense to your brand?

What are the possible consequences of taking this stance?

Existing Business Owners:

Have you taken a stance with your brand?

Could adding some industry-related controversy help your business gain visibility or market share?

Your Target Market

Let's start this section by defining "target market." Your target market is who you want to work with and who you're going to market to—the specific subset of people who are the kind of people that you are going to craft your brand to attract. Your target market is defined by certain demographic, geographic, psychographic (how they think) and even technographic (how they use technology) characteristics, and by their hobbies, interests, and lifestyle choices.

You *can* have more than one target market, but it's generally best to start out focusing on one basic target market. Once you've successfully reached that group and are meeting their needs, you can expand out to another target market, but it's best to focus on the initial market first.

Why Choose a Target Market?

Choosing a target market can be scary for entrepreneurs. You may be worried that if you narrow your market down too much, you won't have enough business, or you'll miss somebody who wants to do business with you.

Have you ever gotten a gift from someone that tells you that person wasn't thinking of you *at all?* Someone once gave me a pair of wool gloves, which would have been a nice gift...for someone else. I'm not allergic to wool, but I am highly sensitive to it. I've tried every form of wool, even the softest, newest blends, and there is no form of wool that I can wear. And most of my friends know this about me, because they are the annual recipients of wool socks that I *love* to knit, but only make for other people, because I can't wear them.

The person who gave me those wool gloves meant well but was using the worst-ever strategy of gift-giving—giving someone a gift that *you* would want. The best strategy of gift-giving, the way to give someone a gift that they will never return or hide away in a drawer (or worse, re-gift), is to buy them something that he or she wants.

But just imagine if you had to buy a birthday gift for someone using the best strategy of gift-giving, where you wanted to give what the person wanted—only you didn't know who you were buying the gift for, you didn't know any characteristics of the person, you didn't even know what the person wanted. Worse, once you bought whatever gift you were going to buy, you didn't know where to send the gift. It's an impossible scenario, right?

It's just as impossible as *not* choosing a clear target market and trying to create a brand, products, or services to serve...someone. How could you possibly know where to begin?

Your business is a gift. But it's not a gift that everyone in the world needs or that everyone wants (even if *you* think they should). Instead of giving people what you think they'd want or, worse, what you'd like to give them, you need to choose who you're going to give your gift to and get to know that group of people so that you can make your gift into the format that they want most.

To use another metaphor, not choosing a target market is like having a bunch of darts, but no dartboard. Since you don't know the target, you throw the darts wildly, hoping to hit something useful. In real world terms, this is trying all kinds of marketing and advertising efforts, but not seeing results.

What would happen if you had a dartboard and knew *exactly* where to throw the darts? What if you knew how to hit that target every single time? In real world terms, your small business will be *far* more successful if you know exactly who you want to serve, where to find those people, and what they want, so that you can give it to them.

> " Your business is a gift. But it's not a gift that everyone in the world needs or wants (even if you think they should). "

To choose a target market (or hone the one you have), you must face the fear of not being everything to everybody. I've seen this happen in virtually every industry. Many entrepreneurs think if they narrow down their market, by excluding people, they'll lose business.

If you don't narrow your market, you'll have more potential clients, but fewer of them will come to you, because they won't know if you can address their specific needs.

If you *do* narrow your market, you'll have fewer potential clients, but you'll also have a much higher quality of prospective clients. Plus, they'll be more likely to want what you have to offer because you'll have tailored your products and services specifically to their driving needs.

Narrowing a target market or choosing a niche doesn't mean that you can't work with someone outside your target market. You *absolutely* can. For example, my target market for Business in Blue Jeans is (in the broadest, most general sense) small businesses and startup entrepreneurs, but I frequently work with medium-sized businesses in growth and consult for large corporations.

Choosing a target market isn't about *not* working with people; it's about finding a target market that you can really focus on and get to know so you can meet their needs and wants. If someone comes along who is interested in what you have to offer and you want to work with that person, but he or she is not in your target market, that certainly doesn't mean you turn him or her away.

Let me show you how this works for one of the "big boys." Anyone can buy Nike products, but their target market is serious, driven athletes. But if you go to the store and watch who's buying Nike, it's not just people who are serious, driven athletes. It's also people who want to be or wish they were serious, driven athletes. It's also people who just like the way Nike gear looks. But in the checkout line, you don't see cashiers saying, "Oh, no, I'm sorry, you're not in Nike's demographic so you can't buy this."

The point is to choose a clear target market and design your packaging and marketing to attract that group of people, but that doesn't mean you turn away business that's outside your target market.

It's easier to be a big fish in a little pond than to be a little fish in a big pond. If you have a poorly defined target market, you're a little fish in a big pond, and you look like all the other fish. There's nothing to set you apart from any of the other millions of little fish.

If you have a clearly defined target market and you know who you serve, you instantly become a big fish in a little pond, and you stand out more. More importantly, all the creatures in your little pond know that you can help them solve their problems.

Now that you understand why it's so important to choose a target market, let's talk about what constitutes a good target market.

What's a Good Target Market?

Many entrepreneurs think they've chosen a target market if they say, "I work with female entrepreneurs" or "I work with work-at-home-moms," but frankly, that's just not specific enough. At this point, with any one of these descriptions, you're still a little fish in a big pond. (And God forbid you say that your target market is "the world." Even if you're solving world hunger, *the entire world* isn't hungry.)

Your target market needs to get more specific like, "American women, age thirty to fifty-five, living in urban areas who earn $55,000-$75,000 annually, who drive economical cars, who are married and have children, who want to spend more quality time with their families, who own their own homes, and who regularly attend church." And even that probably isn't specific enough! If you think your target market is well-defined enough, chances are it could still be improved.

A target market that isn't very well-defined, say, "professional people in their thirties and forties," doesn't give you enough information to create and support a brand that will draw in the audience you need.

For example, let's say that you're a coach who works with anyone on a variety of issues. You might choose any number of coaching strategies to help people move forward in their lives, in *any* areas of their lives. And you might be great at what you do. But you probably won't be very successful or have very many clients, because you don't have a well-defined target market, it's not clear that you understand your target market, and as a result, you probably haven't crafted a brand that will draw them in.

In fact, if this sounds like you, I'd be willing to bet that when you chose the name of your company, you focused more on expressing *your point of view* rather than drawing in your target market.

On the other hand, you'll be a lot more successful if your target market is this specific: "women in their thirties and forties who are in the healing industry, and who are mid-level in their careers with a fairly full client load, but who are interested in continuing education, who have families and busy lives, and who exercise regularly. The health of their clients *and* taking care of themselves are priorities. Their driving needs are seeking balance, time management, and stress relief. What keeps them up at night is the stress of not knowing if they'll have enough time to work with their clients and make dinner for their families at the same time."

If your target market was that specific, you'd probably also have a business name and brand that was specifically designed to attract these women into your business and to convey to them that you know *exactly* how to help them. Your products and services would be designed to meet their deepest, most driving emotional needs and to provide them with answers to their biggest questions and solutions to their most pressing problems.

When you have a clearly defined target market, you know who they are, what matters to them, what keeps them up at night, and what they need help with. You know what will appeal to them, and you know where to find them.

From this point forward, *everything in your business can flow*. That doesn't mean there won't be frustrating moments, but everything will feel different, because you'll have a clear path to follow. Choosing a target market and getting clarity with that target market defines your path—with your brand, with your marketing, and with your offerings.

You don't want to be an "everyman brand." Potential customers and clients won't be one hundred percent certain that you're right for them or that you understand their needs. When you're an "everyman brand," nothing differentiates you from all of your competitors in the marketplace.

Defining Your Target Market

Much of the process of defining your target market goes back to your fire and your expertise. The sweet spot where those two areas merge may provide a key to the direction to head in.

However, if you're like me, your sweet spot may not give away all the answers. My sweet spot includes writing, speaking, teaching, and business. There are a number of directions I could go in with that sweet spot, so I had to narrow down what I really loved most about the things in that sweet spot and who I most enjoyed working with.

Who Do You Like?

If your sweet spot doesn't give you the answers, then ask who you *like* working with. Much of your target market selection is based on your choice and who you enjoy working with the most. This step focuses on identifying when *you* feel the happiest, when you feel the most passionate about what you do, and when you're really making a difference. You're choosing a target market that fits *you*. It's your business, after all, and you get to work with people you *like*.

Ask yourself who you like working with and who you're comfortable working with. As you're answering this

> **From this point forward, everything in your business can flow. That doesn't mean there won't be frustrating moments, but everything will feel different, because you'll have a clear path to follow.**

question, notice any limiting beliefs that may emerge. This can be a tricky moment. Self-worth issues really get in the way of the choice you make here.

The 80/20 Rule

If you're already in business, look at the top twenty percent of your client base—the twenty percent of your clients who generate the most income for you and/or the twenty percent you like working with the most. What do those people have in common? This provides you with a starting point.

Of course, the degree to which you can choose your target market is relevant to your industry. As a coach or consultant, or even a dentist, for example, you'd have a lot more choice over who your market is than, say, a bikini manufacturer.

Who Wants Your Sweet Spot?

(Oh, boy, doesn't that sound dirty? You know I don't mean it like that!)

You may not have a list of products and services yet. But you know what your sweet spot is. So who wants what you have in that sweet spot, and who's willing to pay for it?

Depending on your industry, who wants what you want to offer and who can pay for it may be a more important, determining factor than your choice of who you like working with.

Consider my husband's custom drum-building company. Leo knew he wanted to build drums, so obviously his target market was "drummers." But it wasn't until he drew his line in the sand and decided to honor the "Made in U.S.A." label in its purest form that he realized there was more to the story.

The more research Leo did into using American components, the more he realized that he would be using artisans and craftsmen to create the components. That meant he was going to create a higher quality drum, one with better sound and more appeal to a higher caliber of drummer. Leo was more than happy for his company to create superb instruments, so he didn't really have to choose between who he wanted to work with and who wanted what he was going to offer, because they were one and the same.

Your goal is to find who wants what you have to offer. Then, from among those people, choose who you'd like to serve the most.

If you're interested in an online audience, you can use a combination of online tools to find out what people are searching for and how much they're searching (see http://BusinessInBlueJeans.com/book for the latest tools that I'm using). This can give you a sense of whether there's a true online market for what you bring to the table. From there you can start to define your target market more clearly.

Assessing Your Target Market

You'll need to answer a few questions to make sure you've found a target market that will help you grow your business.

Does your target market want what you have to offer?

We'll talk more about this in the section on "Offerings" (remember The Interplay; this process goes back and forth), but what you need to know is, do they want that sweet spot? Will you need to educate them to understand the value of what you have to offer? An audience that already knows what you have to offer is of use to them is an audience that will be much easier to sell to than an audience that has to be convinced that your product or service is worthwhile.

Can the target market you've defined afford to buy your products and services?

Remember early on, when you planned your whys and put a dollar figure to your dreams? Knowing your goals is useful in this process because that dollar figure number can affect the choices that you make now.

You can build a business two ways: on *pricing*, where you increase your prices and make more by charging more, or on *volume*, where you keep your prices low, but make money by selling a bunch of what you have to offer. How you build your business depends on your business model, your target market, and the products you're offering, as well as a few other factors.

If you're going to choose a target market without many resources, you'll have to be willing to sell at a lower price and build your business on volume.

Think carefully about your target market. Find out if they can afford what you're going to offer. Don't get hung up on general economic conditions or what you *think* they can afford. Get in there and do the research so you *know*.

As you answer these questions, *don't assume* anything about your target market. Do the research and find out, but bear in mind that even in an anonymous survey, people won't always tell you the truth. Sometimes the responses you get in a survey are biased because people tell you what they think the "right" answer is or what they wish was true. The most honest voting that people do is with their dollars.

Still, talk to the people in your target market and get a clear sense of what's out there and if they *really* can afford to buy your products and services.

Are there enough of them out there to sustain you?

There's a delicate balance here: If you've defined a target market too narrowly, then there may not be enough people in that market to sustain you and your business. On the other hand, if you've defined it well, you'll find plenty of business.

A COMMENT ON THE COACHING INDUSTRY

If you're a coach, defining your target market can be a little tricky. The coaching industry has proliferated in the last ten years or so. Back in the days when I launched my coaching business, there weren't many of us out there. But today, there are tens of thousands of coaches. And while coaching started out as a success industry, today around eighty-five percent of coaches make less than $20,000 a year.

The reason it's important to highlight the true state of the coaching industry today is so you know that to be a successful coach, you have to create a brand that will speak to your target market and tell them who you are, who you help, what you do for them, and how you do it.

There's *plenty* of business to go around. Coaching is an extraordinarily valuable service that can change lives. And since there are so many coaches who *aren't* defining themselves and who are out there saying the same things as every other coach, you have a huge opportunity *if* you create something that really stands out.

HOMEWORK ASSIGNMENT:
DEFINING YOUR TARGET MARKET

Newbies:

Answer these questions:

1. Who do you love working with?

2. Who wants what you have to offer (what's in that sweet spot of your business)?

3. Who can pay for what you want to offer?

Write a thorough description of your target market.

Existing Business Owners:

Answer these questions:

1. Who's in the top twenty percent of your client base?

2. Is your target market defined well enough? If not, work on improving your target market definition.

Understanding Your Target Market

Once you've defined your target market clearly, get to know them. You should know them almost better than they know themselves. Everything in your business flows from this point forward. Knowing your target market means you can create products and services that appeal to them, design a brand that attracts them, and develop marketing campaigns that draw them in.

Remember how I said that not choosing a target market is like throwing darts without a dartboard? Well, not understanding your target market is like throwing darts at a dartboard but having poor vision. If you know who you're marketing to, but you don't know anything about them, you *still* won't be able to hit the target.

The Important Data

Once you've chosen a good target market, you need to know every piece of data you can glean about them. How old are they? Where do they live?

Where do they shop? What do they read? How often do they exercise? How do they connect with others? There are many pieces of this puzzle, and you need to find them all and figure out how they fit together. Get inside the heads of your target market and discover who these people are, how they think, and what they worry about.

> **Not understanding your target market is like throwing darts at a dartboard but having poor vision. If you know who you're marketing to, but you don't know anything about them, you still won't be able to hit the target.**

Will everyone in your target market like the same TV shows? Probably not, but there will be trends and patterns that you can spot. From this information, you should be able to build a profile of your ideal client and anticipate your customers' needs.

Building a Profile

Some companies have profiles of their ideal client or customer. I've heard many times that Volvo has a very specific profile of their ideal car buyer. It's said that she's in her mid-thirties, has a college degree, is a mother of two children, is environmentally conscious…the description goes on and on and is highly precise. According to one profile I read, Volvo even gave her a name.

Every time they consider a change, whether it's to the cars themselves or to a marketing campaign, they ask themselves how this specific woman would react to the adjustments. Likewise, you can build a profile of your ideal client or customer to serve in a similar way.

A word of caution, however: Many of my clients who started their businesses to fill a need *they* had, thought they could simply describe themselves in order to create the ideal customer profile.

Even if you are in your own target market, do try to go deeper than just what *you* want. Working within the "I am my own ideal client" framework tends to become far too insular. Plus, you're rarely your own target market, even if you think you are. Get outside your own head and do the research!

The "Point of Pain"

The most important thing that you need to understand is your target market's "point of pain"—that thing that keeps them up at night. Their point of pain is the most significant piece of information you can glean. What are their fears, their worries? What keeps them awake at night or causes their anxiety?

Once you know what keeps your target market up at night the most, how they think about that problem, and what their attitude is about solving it, you can craft a brand that shows you can meet their needs, develop products and services that solve their biggest challenges, and create extremely effective marketing plans. Because you'll know this audience inside out, you can also design a customer experience from top to bottom that will have your clients telling everyone they know about you.

You Can't Make This Stuff Up

You can't make up the data on your target market. You have to dive into the deep end and ask. If you have a mailing list, asking is easy. Create a survey and invite the folks on your list to participate. Give them a gift to thank them for their time and willingness to share with you.

If you're not in business or you don't have a list, you can create an online survey using a free tool (visit the book web site for some resources: http://BusinessInBlueJeans.com/book). Ask friends who fit into your target market to participate in your survey. Go into discussion boards, forums, and social media groups where your target market is likely to be and see if you can find people who are willing to take your survey. Don't post the same content to a ton of groups, because that comes across like spam and is likely to turn everyone off. Instead, approach each group individually and get a sense for the culture of each group before you post. You may even want to contact the group organizer and ask if she or he will help you by posting the survey link for you.

> **You can't make up the data on your target market. You have to dive in and ask. A lot of your success comes from talking to the people you want to market to so that you can address real needs and desires.**

Get enough feedback to know if you're heading in the right direction. If you only have five to ten responses to a survey, you can't really say you know your target market. It's better to have fifty to one hundred responses so you can gauge their reactions and get to the core of their driving needs.

Even though this research may seem like a lot of effort, it pays off. In the long run, a lot of your success comes from talking to the people you want to market to so that you can address real needs and desires.

"The Ten"

When you want to know what resonates with your target market, it's best to ask them. Generally speaking, data is only valid when it's collected from over a hundred people. That said, finding a hundred people can be challenging and time consuming if you're a small business owner. In that case, a focus group can be an acceptable alternative, as long as you understand that the data you get won't be 100 percent reliable.

If you're truly pressed for time and resources, assemble what I call "The Ten." The Ten is a focus/advisory group of ten individuals, groups, or businesses that are representative of your target market. The goal of The Ten is to be a built-in focus group that you can invite to share feedback on concepts for your business. The Ten is intended to be a temporary group—try to refresh your group at least every year (large corporations use fresh focus groups every time they need them; again, this requires time and resources that you may not have).

One of my clients created a coaching business to work with women over fifty who wanted to rejuvenate their sex lives. She invite her Ten to her home to give her feedback on everything from logo concepts to product designs. After they gave her their thoughts (provided privately and anonymously via written ballots), she gave them a glass of wine and a dessert to say thank you.

Another client, who was improving her cosmetics line, formed a Twenty, and made things more formal. She'd rent a conference room and bring the Twenty in to test out new eye shadow and lipstick colors, with a rigorous questionnaire and interview process. After the focus group meeting, she'd give each participant a gift from her product line.

Your Ten will give you valuable and useful feedback that will help you improve everything you do. But never forget: You are the final decision-maker. Since you're working with a limited data set, there may be times when you get mixed results or when your Ten gives you feedback that your gut tells you isn't in line with the general market.

HOMEWORK ASSIGNMENT:
UNDERSTANDING YOUR TARGET MARKET

Newbies and Existing Business Owners:

Write out a thorough description of your target market that brings together all of the information you've gleaned from them.

Create a profile of your ideal client or customer.

Create "The Ten" for your business.

Analyzing Your Peers

Let's talk competition. Often, I look to the "big boys" in industry and scale down their strategies to apply to small business, but when it comes to competition, I look at things differently than big companies do.

It's not hard to look to big business—Apple, Sony, Google, Microsoft—for examples of how they treat competition. You've seen how they compete head to head with other companies. You can look at the big boys in any industry and see that they're very aware of what other companies are doing and that they're aggressive about winning the competition. In big business, competition is ruthless.

In small business, however, when you're talking about coaches, consultants, insurance agents, realtors, event planners, expert speakers, authors, service professionals of all kinds, or even products of many kinds, there's no need for the same kind of cutthroat competition.

There might be similarities in what two different companies do. Let's face it, real estate agents who sell high-end residential real estate all sell the pretty much same kinds of things. Dentists all do the same kinds of dental cleanings and fillings. One hammer looks a lot like another. So what makes the difference?

Your *brand* and how you implement that brand makes the difference and sets you apart from others in your industry. Later in this chapter, I'm going to show you how you can capitalize on what sets you apart in your industry so that you can stand out.

For now, just know that each of us (whether you're an individual or a company) has a unique voice, personality, and perspective, and *those* are the things that make us different from everyone else. You'll approach things with a different spirit than everyone else in your industry. Start thinking of yourself as competitor-less, because no one will *ever* do what you do in the exact way that you do it. That said, there *are* others in your industry, and it's good to familiarize yourself with who else is in your field.

> **❝ Start thinking of yourself as competitor-less, because no one will ever do what you do in the exact way that you do it. ❞**

When you're starting your business, analyze your peers and learn everything you can about them. You should know your industry inside out and know who the big names are. Learn what your peers offer to their customers, what they do, how they do it, what they're charging, what their web site keywords are, how people find them…everything.

But once you know all of that information, you can distill it down into the most important pieces of information that you need to run *your* business. Then, once you've found and assessed your peers, practice what I call mental hygiene to filter out any brain junk from the idea of competition and the experience of analyzing your peers. Otherwise, you'll lose sight of your own path.

In small business, comparing yourself to others and fretting over competition is common, but it can be dangerous. Worry too much about what your peers are doing and you'll spend a lot of time feeling like you're chasing everybody else and trying to catch up…and that's a losing game every time.

Finding Your Peers

Finding your peers should be fairly simple if you're well versed in your industry.

You can find your peers by doing a little detective work online. The first step is to make a list of your keywords. Choosing your keywords is mostly common sense. By this point you should have a basic sense of what your business is all about.

If you've never played detective like this before, all you have to do is make a list of words that you associate with your business or your products. Then add to that list all the things someone might put into a search engine to solve that point of pain or their biggest problem. What would they search for to find someone like you?

For example, to find me online, you might put in "Business in Blue Jeans" or "Susan Baroncini-Moe," but *only* if you already know me. If you didn't know me, but wanted to find someone like me, you might search for "business consultant," or "marketing strategist," or you might search "help with marketing," or "how to use social media," or "improve customer service." There are dozens of these search terms.

As my friend Bob Burg is fond of saying, when people are searching for a 1/4-inch drill bit, they're not looking for a 1/4-inch drill. What they're really after is a 1/4-inch hole. Keywords are often the 1/4 hole, so think about the problems people search for help with and how they'd search for your help, and make a list of those keywords and their synonyms.

Once you've compiled a good list of keywords, go to your favorite search engine and search those keywords to find a list of your peers. Use some lesser-used search engines as well to ensure your search is comprehensive, and make a list of the top ten businesses that you think are your real peers.

Current vs. Future Peers

I recommend that you actually make *two* lists. On the first list, include the people who look like they're about at your same level in their business journey. Those are your current peers. Then make another list of people that are a tier or a few tiers above you. Those are your future peers.

For example, if you're a burgeoning event planner, David Tutera should be on your future peers list. If you're near the start of your real estate career, someone like Chris Cortazzo should be on your future peers list. These folks are *not* your current peers. For current peers, look for people who are at around the same place in their business growth as you are.

It's okay to look at the folks at the pinnacle of success in your industry and see what they're doing, but remember that those are your future peers. Right now, if you're not yet at that level, how you grow your business will be different from how your future peers operate.

HOMEWORK ASSIGNMENT:

UNDERSTANDING YOUR PEERS

Newbies and Existing Business Owners:

Make a list of your current peers.

Make a list of your future peers.

Getting a Sense of Your Peers

Once you've made your lists of current and future peers, go to their web sites and start analyzing everything. Look at how they build relationships with their customers and clients (if they do). Look at how they handle their social media, at their brand, at their products and services. Make notes about what you like and don't like and about what you would do differently.

Web Sites

You should be able to get a lot of the information from your peers' web sites. If you can't get contact information or other information you need, that in itself is valuable information to learn from.

You can tell a lot from a web site. I don't want to overstate this, because I _have_ known some really successful people who had crummy, amateur-looking web sites, but in general, this rule holds true: If someone has a web site that looks kind of cheap or like they did it themselves, you can _probably_ assume that they're in the amateur leagues. You can probably assume they are not highly successful. If their site hasn't been updated in a long time, you can also assume that they're not very successful. That's good to remember for yourself, too, because that's how your audience will see you.

A SIDE NOTE ON WEB SITES

Even though you're probably not in the same league as Pepsi, Yamaha, Target, Tony Robbins, David Tutera, or any of the other big boys, your web site kind of *is*. That's the thing about branding and web sites: You're going up against the big boys whether you want to or not.

When people visit your web site, they'll compare it to other web sites that they've seen, even the ones for people who are more successful or further along in their careers. That's why you want your web site to look professionally made. If your site looks homemade, then your business won't be perceived as first rate or professional.

Let's say you meet someone at a networking event, and you make a good impression. As soon as that person is back at the office, the first thing he or she will do is pull up your web site. If you've presented as successful and professional in person, but your web site looks like your nephew or friend made it for you, that's not going to jibe with the professionalism that you've exhibited.

This discrepancy creates dissonance in the mind of your potential customer. You've shown a professional façade in person, but your web site is in disharmony with the facade that you presented in person, which creates confusion in the mind of your potential client.

A confused visitor to your web site is never a buyer. People who are confused don't buy, so you're going to lose business if your web site doesn't match how you present yourself in person.

Plus, people feel more comfortable doing business with companies that seem stable. Like it or not, if your web site looks unprofessional and like you don't know how to edit it or you've used a site builder or an automated service to create it, then people aren't going to feel too safe or too comfortable giving you their money.

Finally, one more reason you want your web site to look professionally made is that your web site should be functional and convert visitors to buyers.

So what are you looking for in a web site? How can you tell if someone is successful? First, look at the site overall. If it's a retail site, compare it to a retail site you know. Look at Amazon, Barnes & Noble, or Best Buy and get a feel for what it is that makes those sites so popular and look so successful and organized. Compare "personality web sites" (those for personal brands) to the sites that big name brands that you know are using—they're usually designed well, organized, and easy to use. Finally, compare the site to the companies and people you know who are successful.

To be successful, a web site doesn't have to look *exactly* like those sites, but get a sense of whether or not it's even close or if it's well designed. And remember, all of this should be taken with a grain of salt. I know two very successful guys who have web sites that are really out of date and poorly designed. You *can* be successful and have a crummy web site, but that's the exception more than the rule.

I also use online tools to get a sense of how much traffic a web site is getting (check the book web site for specific resources http://BusinessInBlueJeans.com/book). Traffic can be an indicator about how successful someone is, because if your web site gets traffic, it means a lot of people see what you have to say, and some of those people will likely make purchases.

There are specific features of a web site that will tell you if people have their act together. Look for things like clear terms and conditions, privacy policies, and their contact information. Smart, successful businesses post this information on their web sites and make it fairly easy to find.

Systems

Look at the systems of your competitors. Does it appear that they have systems in place? Can you find their customer service, a way to make returns, information about shipping? If they're a service-oriented business, is it easy to hire them or to find out how to hire them? What you're looking for is whether you can tell if this business has its act together, knows what it's doing, and has plans in place to make sure each customer is served well.

PACKAGING

Products and Services

Look at their products and services. What kind of products do they offer, and what's the quality of their products? Look for authenticity and try to see beyond marketing hype. What are their services, and how do they deliver them? What's your experience going through the web site?

With a product-driven business, you'll find it easier to glean information than you will with a service-oriented business. You can still gather a lot of useful material in a service business, but it may be more challenging.

Social Media

You used to be able to determine how successful someone was by checking them out on various social media sites. You could go to Facebook and see that they were close to their 5,000 friend limit, had a bunch of subscribers and fans, and tell that they were doing pretty well. Or you could look at Twitter and see if they have thousands and thousands of followers, which would be an indication that you were looking at the real deal.

Unfortunately, social media changed with the emergence of companies that sell social media followers and fans. Suddenly, finding out how real someone was became a lot more difficult. These days, it's not just the number of fans and followers someone has, but rather the *engagement* they have with their audience that matters most. This kind of common sense comes from digging deeper and being a real detective.

If someone has hundreds of thousands of authentic views on YouTube, you'd expect them to have a lot of comments, some of them thoughtful, lengthy, or in-depth, *and* you'd expect the people who view the video to have looked at different videos. We're all different and have different interests, even if we share things in common. So each person *should* have a unique "YouTube footprint." I once did some detective work on a popular YouTube video, to look beyond the high number of views and discovered that most of the people who commented on that video had viewed *the same videos as other people who had commented on that video*. That tells me that someone was paying them to view and comment on those videos.

If someone has hundreds of thousands of authentic followers on Twitter, you should expect to see many of those followers interacting with that person, retweeting, commenting, and so on. On Facebook, it's the same thing.

Become a good detective, and look for telltale signs that people have bought their way to the top. *Don't be fooled by optics.* Always look for engagement and dig deeper for the truth!

Still, even beyond your ability to be a good detective, social media isn't always the best indicator of success. One very successful author that I know has only 640-some followers and friends on Facebook because he uses it solely for his personal relationships. I myself entered the social media landscape pretty late in the game, so my numbers in certain social media spaces aren't as high as they would be if I'd joined the game sooner, but I also spend more time focusing on engagement than numbers-building.

> " These days, in social media it's not the number of fans and followers someone has that indicates their level of success, but rather the level of engagement they have with their audience that matters most. "

One thing that social media *is* useful for is getting a sense of who people's friends are—discovering their "village." Look at their Facebook and Twitter feeds and see who they're talking to and talking about. If they talk to powerful, successful people, *and* those people are talking back, then you know they run in similar circles and, most likely, they're powerful and successful too.

Your Internal Voice

As you examine and evaluate your peers, tap into your internal voice. Listen to your own feedback. A lot of people use this research method to get ideas for ways to set up their business or ways to do things (essentially copying what others in their industry are doing), but that's the exact *opposite* of what I'm recommending. Don't be a copycat!

Instead, use this strategy as a way to tap into your individuality. What do you like? What don't you like? What do you think your target market and the people who follow you will respond well to, and what do you think they won't respond well to at all?

Direct Contact

Don't hesitate to e-mail or call your peers and ask them about what they do, who they do it for, and how much they charge. You can also gather useful data about how they treat callers and customers.

You can conduct this research from two angles. I've heard some of my own peers recommend that you call your peers and act like you're interested in becoming their client or customer. I don't think that's particularly honest or authentic if you're not truly interested in working with them or buying their products. However, you never know what can happen. I once called a peer to do research and ended up finding a fantastic mentor.

You might call in an authentic, honest way, and say: "I'm starting or growing a business like yours, and I wonder if you might have a few minutes to answer a couple of questions?" Maybe they'll help you, and maybe they won't. You never know what can happen. At the least, you'll get some great information just by calling or e-mailing companies to see how they handle the customer experience.

Alone, none of these strategies provide enough information to assess each peer. But by using them together, you'll be able to aggregate data that helps you to get a feel for who they are, who they serve, and how they deliver their products and services.

HOMEWORK ASSIGNMENT:
ANALYZING YOUR PEERS

Newbies and Existing Business Owners:

Assemble the data you've compiled about your peers into some sort of comprehensive report. What are your findings? Summarize what you've learned. What did you learn that you liked? What did you learn that you didn't like?

Product and Service Offerings

Now you know your target market and your peers. Newbies, it's time to decide what products and services you're going to offer. Existing business owners, you're going to evaluate what you offer and determine if you're in need of a revamp.

It's Not About You

I can't tell you how many times clients have come to me with the problem that nobody was buying the product they'd put their heart and soul into. It's heartbreaking, really. But more often than not, they could have prevented this problem from the start.

If you create a product based on what *you* think your target market needs (or that the world needs), you're making a grave mistake. Buyers don't buy what *you* want them to buy or even what *you* think they need. They buy what *they* think they need and what *they* want to buy. You can't change the world if the world isn't interested in the change you think the world should make.

> **Buyers don't buy what you want them to buy or even what you think they need. They buy what they think they need and what they want to buy.**

If you have a product that you think your target market needs and/or that you absolutely must create to express some higher purpose or vision, you can still create it. But if you want people to buy it, either you have to find a target market that wants what you're determined to create, or you have to find a way to incorporate what your target market wants.

If you created a product or wrote a book that meant the world to you but didn't sell, I feel your pain. I really do. But now you need to revisit where that thing came from and whether it can be retrofitted to appeal to your target market.

Brainstorming

When you contemplate the products and services you want to offer, the possibilities are endless. To make this process less overwhelming, use the knowledge you've gained about your target market to narrow down the possibilities.

Teaching someone how to brainstorm and how to come up with ideas for products and services isn't easy. In fact, like creating an amazing brand, brainstorming is something that you're either great at or something you're not so great at. Brainstorming new products and services can be frustrating, which is why you may want to hire someone to help you with this process.

Sometimes you're too enmeshed in your industry to see outside the box and to know what the alternatives are. If you can't see beyond the normal, everyday things that people are already creating in your industry and are having a hard time coming up with ideas, bring in someone with an outside perspective and an expertise in product and service development (and these days, a background in understanding what's possible in technology) to help you come up with fresh, new ideas.

When you develop ideas for products, establish a judgment-free brainstorming zone. No idea is a stupid idea in this zone. No idea gets thrown out. Brainstorming is a time to be completely free and to think creatively. Wild, extravagant, and grandiose ideas, ideas that might be completely impossible...everything is fair game. During brainstorming, your goal is to generate a large number of ideas that you can sift through later.

A NOTE ON TEAM BRAINSTORMING

Counter to what you might think, team brainstorming can actually generate *fewer* ideas than independent brainstorming. If you have to use team brainstorming, have team members brainstorm ideas independently *before* coming to a group brainstorming session. Reserve group time for expanding on the ideas individuals bring to the table. After the group brainstorming session, have team members brainstorm independently again.

As you think about the possibilities, allow your mind to roam. Look at all mediums and formats without limitations. Consider things you've seen before and could make better. Think about different ways to solve problems or express the solutions you provide. Expand your thinking outside the realm of your own industry and look at how other industries do things. Innovations often happen by drawing inspiration from other industries into your own—what's old hat in another industry becomes new and fresh in yours.

Once all the brainstorming is over, sift through the ideas you've generated and start assessing and critiquing them. Which ideas are innovative and fresh? What will appeal to your target market?

This is a great opportunity to go back to your "Ten" and get their feedback on your ideas.

Product Research

Once you've narrowed down your ideas, it's always a good idea to do your research to find out if a product that you want to create is already out there. If it is, find out everything about the products that exist. Can you improve on them or innovate to make them better?

I've had clients who had an idea for a product innovation and, upon discovering a product already existed, ordered one of each of those existing products to compare their solution with what was already on the market. These comparisons can also help you create marketing materials later.

Product Planning

If you can improve what's out there, begin to outline what you're going to offer and create a plan for the creation of your product. If you're going to offer a tool, what will it do? Who do you need to help you create it?

If you're working on an invention or a new product, you may need to have a prototype made before you can even come up with a budget for the business itself. Without a prototype, you may not even be able to find out how much production, packaging, and shipping will cost, so you can't set a retail price, set up cost or timeline projections for the business, or anything else. The options to get a prototype made are endless—from making it yourself to having a local craftsman hand-machine something to "rapid prototyping" (which, despite the name, can still take several months from sketch to 3D CAD drawing to actual polymer prototype).

HOMEWORK ASSIGNMENT:
PRODUCT AND SERVICE DEVELOPMENT

Newbies:

Begin brainstorming products and services that you can offer in your business.

Do you want to create a product of your own or sell items others have created?

If you want to create your own product, is it a tangible product (something your customers can touch) or a digital product?

If you want to sell items that others create, what kinds of things do you want to sell?

Do you want to offer services?

What kinds of services do you want to offer?

Are there other outside-the-box ways to deliver the services that you want to offer?

Existing Business Owners:

Examine your existing product and service offerings.

How can you expand on what you're already delivering?

If you offer tangible products or in-person services, are there ways to transform what you offer into digital products or web-based services?

Are there other outside-the-box ways to deliver what you're offering?

Your Business Model

Now that you have a mission statement, and have chosen a target market, checked out your peers, founded your focus/advisory group, and begun to develop your products and services, it's time to get serious about creating your business model.

What *is* a business model? At its most fundamental, your business model is how you deliver value to your target market.

For example, a retail store that relies mostly on foot traffic through a local mall is built on a "bricks and mortar" business model. In contrast, a retail store that sells to foot traffic as well as online is built on a "bricks and clicks" model. If you're a coach or consultant who charges for your services, then you have a fee-based business model. There are numerous business models, but what's most important is that you choose the business model that makes the most sense for your target market and the products and services you want to deliver.

Will you find most of your customers and clients online? Or will you find them another way? Start with where your target market is and how they're going to find you, and then move on to the best way to deliver your products and services.

Delivering Products and Services

Products and services can be delivered in many different ways these days. You can write a book that gets published by a big, well-known publisher and sold in bricks and mortar stores. You can write a book, put it into digital format, and sell it as an e-book on Amazon or iTunes. You can teach a workshop in person to twenty-five people, or you can hold a webcast and teach thousands. You can sell DVDs, or you can sell downloadable videos. The universe of products and services today is almost unlimited.

With all this possibility, how do you decide what to offer to your potential customers and clients? This is an answer you'll hear me say over and over and over again: Go back to the information you've gathered about your target market.

Do the people who you want to serve prefer tangible books with pages they can turn, or do they prefer to read digital books? Do the people in your target market like to pop in a DVD and settle back on the sofa, or do they want to watch videos from you on their laptops?

It's also important to know your industry. How are other companies in your industry delivering products and services to your target market? Is there a reason why these companies deliver in that way, or has no one in the industry yet innovated delivery?

Some products can't be turned into digital commodities, and some products can only be delivered in one way. Obviously, a bakery can only deliver cakes and cookies in a real, tangible form. You can't turn delicious confections into a digital product (if only!). But you *can* turn the selling of them into a digital service.

Teaching and Membership Models

Let's say that you *are* a bakery and you want to reach a geographic market that extends beyond your local neighborhood. First, you can innovate with delivery by offering online ordering and delivery to a wider area. But what if you wanted to find a way to deliver digitally? How could you do that?

By *teaching* people how to make their own delicious treats. You could, for example, offer an online class, where each month you teach people a new recipe or technique via video. Members of the program would get free shipping on any order and a discount on the treat you're teaching them to make that month. So if you taught them to make a special toffee cookie (my personal favorite) this month, then you give them a discount to buy *your* toffee cookies, because really, no matter how well you teach them, they'll never make cookies as good as yours. And who has time to make cookies anyway?

Club Scrap

The last fifteen years or so brought a massive wave of scrapbooking frenzy. People everywhere began clamoring to put their photos into complex, well-designed, crafty scrapbooks. Scrapbooking stores cropped up, classes filled up, and I think it's fair to say that scrapbooking became a craze.

The challenge in scrapbooking is finding papers and accessories and putting them together into a cohesive look. You can spend literally *hours* in a crafting store trying to find exactly the right papers, stamps, stickers, and all *kinds* of other stuff to make your scrapbook perfect (this is why I can't be a scrapbooker—it's not a good hobby for people who aren't good at design or who have perfectionist tendencies).

Club Scrap, started in 1999 by Trisha, a talented scrapbooker, and Dinah, an incredible graphic designer, took a lot of the scrapbooking challenge, where you spend all that time trying to find just the right collection of pieces to make an incredible book, and made it simple. They assemble coordinating papers, tools, stickers, eyelets, fibers, all *kinds* of things, into kits that they pack with instructions and send to their members each month in white pizza boxes. Then, if members want additional papers or supplies, they simply order them (at a discount, of course).

The genius of Club Scrap is that it's a monthly kit (so, continuing revenue for the company and continuing enjoyment for the members) that takes the painful work out of scrapbooking and paper crafts and leaves only the fun part for its monthly members to enjoy. Plus, they're driving additional sales of extra supplies at the same time. It's win-win for everyone!

Bespoke Post

Bespoke Post is another membership program that caters to a masculine demographic. Each month, Bespoke Post sends a "Box of Awesome" to their members, who get to choose from two or three different boxes. Past boxes have included aged cocktail kits, the best in shaving accessories, and meat curing sets.

There are all *kinds* of ways to riff on this business model. One of my clients is a former nanny who helps parents improve their parenting skills. She started a monthly program with a starter kit that includes the necessities she believes each parent needs; then each month she adds a new tool or activity or something else that parents can use to enhance their relationship with their kids.

The monthly membership model works with digital products, too. I've run monthly membership programs where each month my members get to participate in a phone call with a business leader like Jack Canfield or Jack Trout and then ask their own questions. I've had other programs where each month I teach my members a new marketing strategy or bring in one of my expert friends to teach a useful webinar. The ways in which you can use a monthly membership model are almost endless.

Turn Your Industry on Its Ear

As you're developing products and services and pondering your business model, get creative! Think about all the ways in which you can change your industry around, offer products and services in new and different ways, or turn the business models you already know on their ears.

Save The Date

My friend Jennifer Gilbert, Chief Visionary for Save the Date, is an ingenious event planner. When the event planning industry was struggling, Jennifer found a way to turn the industry's known business model on its ear to keep her company afloat.

Most event planners would charge a flat fee for planning an event, and the person hosting the event paid for their services as well as for the facility rental, the catering, the furniture, and everything else. When the economy hit a bump and event hosts found themselves having a hard time paying for event planning services, Jennifer knew she needed to do something different to survive.

So she started offering her services to event hosts for free, but had the service providers (the venues, caterers, etc.) pay her a percentage of what they earned. This completely changed the industry and kept Save the Date in business when many event planning companies went under.

By challenging assumptions about your industry, you may find a new way to offer your services and products in a way that no one has done before and, in the process, just might set yourself apart from your peers.

> " **By challenging assumptions about your industry, you may find a new way to offer your services and products in a way that no one has done before.** "

Be Open to the Possibilities

As you choose your business model, be conscious of all of the options and possibilities. Open your mind and consider all the ways in which you can offer products and services. It's a new world, and you're not just limited to what you've seen before.

Borrow from other industries. Try on different options and see how they fit you and your target market. Some things simply won't work in certain industries, but you won't know unless you open your mind to the potential available opportunities.

HOMEWORK ASSIGNMENT:
YOUR BUSINESS MODEL

Newbies and Existing Business Owners:

Describe your business model in its entirety.
Where will you find your customers and clients?
How will they find you?
What's the best way to deliver your products and services?
How do you charge your clients and customers?
Are there ways to innovate on what your industry currently does?

PACKAGING YOUR SWEET SPOT INTO A BRAND

Now that you know who your target market is, you've analyzed your peers, started to create or analyze a list of products and services, and have a sense of your business model, you can begin to create your brand.

What the Heck Is "Branding" Anyway?

You hear *branding* all the time in business—you're supposed to create a fantastic brand, increase brand awareness, have a brand identity, even create a brand bible...but what the heck *is* branding, anyway?

A Brief History Lesson

Branding, as a term, originated with the Old Norse word *brandr,* meaning "to burn." The concept as we know it today probably originated with the practice of early cowboys using hot irons to sear their initials onto the flank of their cows, to make sure everyone knew which cows belonged to which ranches.

The Industrial Revolution brought the advent of non-local goods being shipped to small towns, where previously the townspeople only had access to local products that were made by people they knew. In order to compete with trusted local producers, mass-market manufacturers created identities (or brands) for their products. Some of these early brands were Aunt Jemima and Campbell's soup. Creating brands allowed out-of-town manufacturers to convince people that their products were just as trustworthy as the locally made ones.

After 1900, branding took off, so that by the 1940s, companies were thinking about branding much in the way that we do today, by looking at the personality of the brand and how it was embodied through slogans, logos, and mascots. That's when companies started looking at how consumers related to their brands in psychological and sociological ways.

So What Is Branding?

Today branding is the creation of an image and identity for a product, service, or company that, when encountered by the consumer, forms a comprehensive experience for that person.

I've talked about Nike already, largely because it's a recognizable brand and because their branding is so clear. If you close your eyes and think of what the Nike brand represents, do you see the images of athletes sweating and pushing themselves past their limits of physical endurance? Most of us do…and that's a big part of what branding does: It creates that experience in our mind's eye.

Think about Apple. When you think about the technology and products they create, it's not just about being the fastest or best-performing technology. It's about having an edge, a design, something that makes

> **Branding isn't just a name or a style, it's everything that happens in your business, from start to finish.**

them cooler, hipper, and even a little more tech-savvy than everybody else. That's why there's a character in our culture we refer to as an "Apple person."

Branding creates recognizability, *and* it creates an experience in the mind of the consumer, which you hope leads them to either connect with the brand (as in, "That's me!") or to *want* to be the person who connects with the brand (as in, "That's who I want to be!").

So branding isn't just a name or a style, it's *everything* that happens in your business, from start to finish. Your products and service say something about your brand. Your customer service says something about your brand. It's *all* a part of your brand.

Why Does Branding Matter to My Small Business?

Branding matters to your small business because you want to reach your target market effectively so they know that you exist and can make their lives better.

Branding matters to your small business because your target market wants to be assured that you know and understand their needs and that buying from you will provide something for them.

Branding matters to your small business because you want to stand out in the marketplace so that the world notices you and your company will grow.

The fact that we're all so interconnected in today's market, though, means that in many ways your brand is competing side by side in the marketplace with giant corporations like Target and Apple and Nike and Coca-Cola. So your brand needs to be just as awesome, which is one of the challenges of creating a brand as a small business.

Bear in mind that large corporations have millions to spend on research and development of new brands. They don't always get it right, but they can usually afford a mistake here and there. Some, however, can't.

As of the writing of this book, there are three major office chains in the United States: Staples, Office Depot, and OfficeMax. If you were to stand in any of those stores, you'd be hard-pressed to tell which one you're in. All three stores have red logos, and there's no difference in pricing, staffing, customer service, product lineup, reward programs, or anything else. There's almost no reason for any consumer to be loyal to *any one* of these stores. I'll be amazed if all three of these triplets are still standing by the time this book comes out in paperback.

A major branding mistake can have significant consequences, regardless of whether you're a giant business or a small business. But in big business, a branding "hiccup" can be managed. In small business, however, a branding mistake can cost you everything.

On the upside, however, there are some benefits to being a small business when it comes to branding. While large corporations often have multiple product lines, each with its own brand identity, small businesses typically have just one overarching brand that represents their company in the marketplace. That makes your life simpler.

Plus, small businesses can choose between a personal brand (if, for example, my company was just called "Susan Baroncini-Moe") or a brand identity (as in "Business in Blue Jeans"). That means you have options.

Creating (or Revamping) the Brand Identity

For Existing Business Owners: When to Revamp a Brand Identity

I can't tell you how many business owners I've talked to over the years who have said things like,

"I made my own logo and business card. It'll do for now."

"When I'm more successful, I'll invest in a really good logo."

"Someday I'll be able to afford a web site for my business."

"I don't need a fancy logo or business card for what I do."

"My business is small. I don't need much of a brand."

If you've said these things, your brand probably needs to be revamped.

When you go out into the marketplace, no matter who your target market is, remember, you're competing with other companies—and not just others in your industry or other businesses the same size as yours.

These days we're bombarded with so much information and so many marketing messages that our brains simply don't differentiate small companies from big ones. So consumers instinctively compare your logo to those of the big companies like IBM, T-Mobile, and Honda. And how do you think you stack up if you cobbled your logo together using clip art?

> **If your brand identity is clear in conveying what you do and who you do it for, you'll attract the right clients and customers.**

One giant mistake small business owners make is putting off brand identity development until they think they can afford it. But there are many reasons why brand development is important *now*.

If your brand identity is clear, then you'll be clearer in conveying what you do and who you do it for, so that you'll attract the right clients and customers—people who want what you have and are willing to pay for it.

Right now, think about your corporate identity and your brand. What's the brand that you're putting out there? What do you do, and who do you do it for? Do your services and pricing match up with the brand you've created?

Do you find clients who want what you have and are able to pay for it? If not, first look at your target market—who do you want to work with, and are you attracting those people? Then look at the message you're sending—does the message you're sending match with the clients or customers you want to attract?

Do you have a logo (and a web site) that has been professionally designed, not something you made yourself? How does your company look next to big corporations? I'm not saying you have to look as big as they look, but you should look professional and serious about your business.

You can't wait until your business is successful to make it *look* successful. After all, who would you rather work with, a company that looks reputable and serious and professional or someone who looks like they're just starting out and may or may not be in business in six months? Make your business *look* successful in order to *become* successful.

Sometimes the issue may be as simple as a brand styling issue. Maybe you're sending conflicting messages. Do the visual aspects of your brand identity (like your logo) make sense with the name of your business?

Many years ago, I had a client who came up with a very cool name for her new business, but the name was extremely feminine. When she chose the logo, though, she went against my advice (gasp!) and chose a corporate-looking logo that didn't go with her brand *at all*. As a result, she sent a really conflicting, confusing message to her audience. And as you know by now, a confused buyer never buys. Sadly, that client's business never really got off the ground, and her brand styling was a large part of the reason why.

If you're not sure if your brand needs revamping, ask your Ten or hire a consultant who can help you decide if revamping the brand is what's needed to grow your business.

As you work on the brand for your business, you must have absolute clarity with regard to what your company is, what you stand for, what you're going to deliver, and who your target market is. If you haven't done the homework assignments to fully understand your target market and their beliefs, attitudes, and points of pain, then go back and do the assignments now. You must have a complete understanding so that you know what colors and styles appeal to your demographic.

HOMEWORK ASSIGNMENT:
REVAMPING YOUR BRAND

Existing Business Owners:

Critically analyze your brand.

Does your brand styling match up with your brand name, message, and mission statement?

Do you have a logo that looks homemade or one that looks professional?

Are you sending confusing, mixed messages to your target market?

Is it time to revamp or restyle?

PACKAGING

Defining Your Brand

Personal Brand vs. Corporate Brand

I'm often asked by clients if they should design a brand for their business or if they should design a "personal brand," a brand that's based around the owner of the business.

If you're a well-known name, someone famous or a celebrity, then build a personal brand and create products as offshoots from that brand. You can see how this works when you look at celebrities who become entrepreneurs.

In the 1980s, Rikki Rockett was a famous drummer in a band called Poison. These days, Rikki has a drum company called Rockett Drums that plays off of his celebrity brand. Similarly, Jessica Simpson created a massive celebrity brand, which features Jessica Simpson shoes, purses, clothing, and fragrances. Dan Aykroyd created Crystal Head Vodka and is featured in the advertisements and interviews talking about the brand.

On the other hand, some celebrities take a different approach. Sandra Bullock owns a bistro called Bess, where she crafted the entire menu of the restaurant and designed the candles they sell at the counter. While some people know of the celebrity connection, many consumers remain completely unaware.

There's also a way to do this that's a fusion of both strategies.

Mary Kate and Ashley Olsen were the most famous twin actors in the world, and they created a vast empire out of their celebrity brand. But when they wanted to be "taken seriously" as adults, they created fashion lines with completely different brands, The Row and Elizabeth and James. People in the industry know that these brands belong to the Olsens, but in the marketplace, the brands are slightly separated from their celebrity owners.

Looking at the flip side of the fusion strategy, Richard Branson created Virgin first as a record label, then added the Virgin label to all kinds of other industries like mobile phones and an airline. Then, as Virgin grew into an international success, Branson's personal brand emerged.

On a smaller scale, I've followed a similar model. I created Business in Blue Jeans first as a way to reach small business owners and entrepreneurs; then I realized that I had something to say to larger businesses as well. Blue jeans *can* fit into the corporate world, but I decided to keep the Business in Blue Jeans brand as it was and created my personal brand to work with on a consulting basis and to speak to much larger companies.

The question of whether to create a personal or corporate brand first is very much a "chicken or egg" kind of question.

If you're an entrepreneur who is delivering services to your target market (a coach, an accountant, or a lawyer, for example), then creating a professional personal brand is a natural fit. But that doesn't necessarily have to be the case, as you can see with Business in Blue Jeans, where I've offered consulting services to small businesses for years.

If you're creating a product, establishing a corporate brand is often easier, which you can see with Apple, Virgin, or Sony, and that's what happens in most cases. But if you're a designer creating a line, such as Valentino or Michael Kors, you can also put your name to the design. As we've seen with brands like Lucky and L.A.M.B., though, a corporate brand works just as well.

The point is, when it comes to choosing personal branding over corporate branding, there really is no right answer. Create the brand that is most appealing and attractive to your target market and expresses your point of view best.

Personal Branding

So what is personal branding all about? It's about the brand of *you*. Specifically, as my friend John Michael Morgan, author of *Brand Against the Machine*, taught me, personal branding is about your perspective. People want to know your opinions, your thoughts on things. The reason you create a personal brand is that it affords you the flexibility to do a lot of things without compromising or muddying the brand of your business.

A personal brand is about you, your style, your unique way of looking at the world. It's about your story, history, experiences, expertise, and skill set—it's *all* of those things put together. You can't build a brand on skills alone, unless you have a skill set that is so unique and high-demand that hardly anyone has the same skills. But the one thing you have that *no* one else has is *you*.

If you want to see some great examples of personal brands, you really don't have to look too far. Politicians have personal brands, but they're not great examples. The best examples are celebrities. Look at your favorite celebrities over the years—how have they changed? How have they evolved? How have they been the same over time?

When you're looking at celebrities, take note that personal brands *evolve* over time. People often believe that branding is static and unchanging—that's partly why we're always trying so darned hard to get it right. But all you have to do is look at celebrities to see how branding can be ever-evolving.

Ozzy Osbourne went from rabid, bat-head-eating heavy metal Prince of Darkness to beloved, bumbling, befuddled reality TV star. Angelina Jolie went from creepy, brother-kissing, blood-vial-wearing weirdo to stunning matriarch, serious actress, and goodwill ambassador. Robert Downey, Jr. went from Brat Pack to addict to celebrated actor. Branding *can* change, and you *can* make mistakes. People will forgive you.

HOMEWORK ASSIGNMENT:
PERSONAL VS. CORPORATE BRAND

Newbies and Re-branding Existing Business Owners:

Which do you choose, personal brand or corporate brand? Which makes the most sense for your business and for attracting your target market?

The Words That Represent Your Business

The next step in creating your brand is to come up with a list of words that represent you and your business—essentially a list of adjectives and other words that represent the message you want to get across. Some of these are words you might find in your mission statement. Others are just adjectives that describe how you want to be represented to your target market.

For example, do you want your business to come across as corporate and serious? Playful or relaxed? What are other words that represent your brand?

When I was developing the name for the company that became Business in Blue Jeans, I listed words like *durable, relaxed, comfortable, joyful, happy, pleasant.* Would you be surprised to learn that I also included *serious* in my list? I included it because I wanted to convey that, while I enjoy an unstructured, relaxed lifestyle and while I want business to be fun for my clients, I am also *very* serious about business. You can always include words that seem like they don't mix. Sometimes it's that juxtaposition that makes a brand interesting, like with Business in Blue Jeans.

HOMEWORK ASSIGNMENT:
THE WORDS THAT REPRESENT YOUR BUSINESS

Newbies:

Come up with a list of words that represent your business. Even if the words seem like they're in disharmony, include them on the list.

Existing Business Owners:

Come up with a list of words that represent your business.

Compare your existing brand to your list. Does your existing brand and the words you listed match up?

Styling the Brand

Naming Your Business

As we've discussed with personal vs. corporate branding, some businesses do well with the owner's name, as in a law or accounting firm. Some businesses do well with acronyms, like IBM. Other companies succeed with made-up words like Google, or powerful one-word statements like Target.

How do you know what to name your business? How do you know what will resonate with your target market and intrigue them enough to come to your web site, visit your location, hire you, or buy your products?

Naming a business is a multi-step process. You don't want to just brainstorm a cute name with your friends, partners, or family members and leave it at that. You must start where everything in your business should always start: with your target market.

What are the primary concerns of your target market, the ones that you're going to help them with? What problems are you going to solve? Once you have a list of concerns or problems that your target market faces, start coming up with words that are associated with the kind of person or business that your target market would want solving their problems. You're looking for adjectives like *trustworthy, strong, fun, exciting, personable,* and so on.

Ask your target market to supply some of these words. Ask The Ten or create a survey and get as many people to participate in it as you can.

Once you have a list of the words that appeal to your target market, brainstorm some more.

Bring in a thesaurus and look for synonyms of the words your target market gave you and the ones you've come up with yourself. Put these words on 3x5 cards and mix and match to see what combinations inspire you. Brands don't have to make sense as wording, otherwise Yahoo, YouTube, and Google would be out of business (which, as of the writing of this book, they're not). It's the meaning they *convey* that matters.

Naming your business is *not* an easy process. Asking friends for help can yield interesting results or terrible ones. And sometimes when you're working on creative elements like this, you can lose perspective and end up with a list of strange or just plain bad names.

If you're going to ask friends and family for assistance, focus on the feedback of those people you know who are in your target market. If you're designing a business geared toward men, your wife may not know what would appeal to men, while your best male friend might have a more solid response.

Once You Have a Name

Also remember that if you come up with a good name, you still need to do some fact-checking to make sure it's okay to use that name.

Check with the Secretary of State where you live to see if the name is already registered for use. Check the U.S. Trademark and Patent office web site to see if the name is already trademarked. And use a domain name registrar to find out if the name is available.

If you discover the name's not being used in your state and isn't trademarked, but the domain isn't available, that's okay. Sometimes domains have been purchased but aren't being used, and you may be able to buy the domain you want. In that case, you may have to spend some money on it, especially if you're buying from a broker, because they like to charge a *lot* for domain names, which are, for all intents and purposes, "digital real estate."

Negotiation is a key asset in this kind of purchase. Never buy a domain name outright at the asking price. If you keep the conversation with a broker going long enough, you can almost always get a clear picture of where the bottom line is. If you can negotiate with an actual human being who owns a domain name that you want rather than, say, a broker, it's usually easier to get a better price.

When your domain isn't available and it's being held, but for whatever reason you can't spend the money they're asking for it, you still have alternatives. While I don't recommend anything but a .com for businesses, you can play around with names a little bit.

Many years ago, I had a business called PopQuotes. Popquotes.com wasn't available, but pop-quotes.com was available, so I bought that. I backordered popquotes.com, in the hopes that it might become available and I might get it. One day, I got lucky—through technological wizardry, I was able to obtain the domain.

HOMEWORK ASSIGNMENT:
NAMING YOUR BUSINESS

Newbies and Re-branding Existing Business Owners:

Add to the list of words that you began in the last assignment. Now you're adding words that come from your target market.

Take all of the words you've written down and transfer them to 3x5 cards. Mix and match these cards to come up with various combinations. Play around and come up with options that you like. Mess

> with the 3x5 cards until the words lose all meaning and you can just work with sounds and the way the words look together.

A cautionary note: When you develop your business name, put the words together and see what the domain name might look like. The last thing you want is to inadvertently create a disaster domain.

Just imagine what happened to the guy who came up with the slogan, "Choose Spain," only to end up with the domain, "choosespain.com," which, for those of you who can't see it, looks a lot like "chooses pain." I'm sure I don't have to tell you why the names "Auctions Hit" or "Pen Island" were bad choices when they were turned into .com domain names. You can probably work those out for yourself.

Walk Away

Sometimes the naming process can be frustrating. The right name doesn't always come to you immediately.

If you become overwhelmed, walk away. Ninety percent of my best business ideas, especially names, come when I walk away from the drawing board to do something else. I've named businesses while doing laundry, cleaning out my closet, or running on the treadmill. You never know when inspiration will hit.

This is a good strategy to keep in your back pocket for almost any creative task. When you step away and allow your brain to relax, the subconscious takes over and continues to work through the problem. Then, when it comes up with a solution, it'll pop into your conscious brain. Sometimes it happens at the weirdest times and certainly when you least expect it.

> **If you start feeling like things aren't coming naturally or you have to force it, it's good to step away and let your conscious brain rest.**

If you start feeling like things aren't coming naturally or you have to force it, it's good to step away and let your conscious brain rest.

More Cautionary Tales

Remember, branding is the most difficult piece of the business puzzle. Figure this part out and it's smooth sailing from here on out. That doesn't mean everything else is *easy*. It just means that this is the part people typically find the most challenging. I've seen more businesses fail, more entrepreneurs give up, more partnerships break up, all during this specific part of the process.

It's tough because it's creative, and it's tough because there are rules that make for good and bad brands, as you've seen. Naming your business is hard because everyone has an opinion about what you should name your business. (And the ideas are always "cute." Avoid cute like the plague!)

Branding is also inherently, deeply creative and soulful. It requires a certain *je ne sais quoi* that most people either don't have or don't think they have. Most entrepreneurs get insecure when they start thinking about branding because it's just something most people don't do every day. And frankly, most people aren't sure if they're doing it right.

Hang in there. Stay with it. Keep trying. Keep working. Eventually you'll get it. And if you don't, your business will probably fail. No pressure. I'm *kidding!* I'm *kidding!*

When you get frustrated—and you *will* get frustrated—walk away, give yourself a break, and remember your *why*.

Visual Appearance

The visual appearance of your brand includes the components that people can see, including your logo, your web site, and all printed collateral like your business cards, brochures, and other marketing pieces, as well as, heck, even *you*.

Logos

How important is something like a logo? You can never have a logo that's too good. You can certainly have a logo that's too *designed*, but you can never have a logo that's too true to your brand.

Logo mistakes usually fall into three general areas. The first mistake is business owners who don't think they need a logo when they start their businesses or (worse) who design their own logo (variation: they have their nephew/friend/that guy at church design their logo). This is almost always a mistake, unless you're a graphic designer, and sometimes even then.

Having a crummy logo makes you look like you're a poor, starving startup and couldn't afford to do better. Whether or not that's true, it's the *last* thing you want potential customers to think of you.

I can't think of any business where you really *want* your clients and customers to think you're new to the game. More often than not, people choose to do business with people they trust. A big part of trust is based in the belief that you have *experience*. If you look like you don't even know enough to get a decent logo, you've lost a big chunk of trust before you've even started talking. Do you *really* want to handicap yourself from the start? That seems like a poor choice to me.

The second mistake entrepreneurs make is in choosing the *wrong* logo. I've seen super-feminine businesses choose oddly masculine-looking logos. I've seen fun, laid-back companies choose overly corporate logos. There's nothing more disarming or confusing than a logo that doesn't match up with the message of the brand. Remember, a confused buyer never buys.

The third mistake small business owners make with their logos is spending an absolute fortune to get high-end, "corporate identities" created. That's a terrible way to invest in your small business. As of the writing of this book, the last logo I had designed was for my own company, Business in Blue Jeans, and the entire corporate identity, including logo, business card, and letterhead, cost me under $500.

All it takes to get a good logo is the right designer and the right concept. As long as you know what you're looking for and can describe it, you shouldn't need to spend a fortune.

Business Cards

I've read a few articles that say we don't need business cards anymore—that they're an outdated investment and just get tossed in a drawer somewhere anyway. While it *might* be true that business cards are on the way out, not having them is still a mistake.

I use business cards all the time, even though I rarely, if ever, attend networking events. For example, I'm writing this chapter from a bar in Indianapolis where my husband is about to play in a live blues jam. When he was on stage last week, a guy recorded the performance. I knew my husband would want to see the video, so I wrote a few notes on my business card and, in between sets, asked the guy with the camera to send me the link, handing him my business card. The next morning, I had a link in my inbox, a new subscriber on Facebook, and someone who wanted more information about what I do...all from giving out that one card.

Of course, that's just one instance. In the aggregate, yes, business cards are silly, especially in the digital age. But if you're doing business and you don't have a business card, you look silly and unprofessional to most businesspeople. You appear as if you don't have your act together, which is the last thing you want people to think about you when you're building trust.

Maybe you can get away with the "I don't believe in business cards" line if you're a rogue like Mark Zuckerberg (for the record, I don't actually know if "Zuck" uses or likes business cards), but most people can't go that direction. For most businesses, having a business card is a must.

Even if you've decided to take a stand against business cards for eco-friendly or digital reasons, do you really have time to stand there and tell a serious businessperson about that stance? Get your business cards printed on recycled paper. It's easier, and it'll play better.

You

You represent your brand. Yes, *you!* That means every time you're out in the world and every time you speak to someone on the phone, you represent your brand. The first thing that means is that you have to be nice to people.

Somewhere a long time ago, I read that the true measure of a person's character can be seen in the way they treat their server in a restaurant. That's also true of the checkout girl at the grocery store, the teller at the bank, and the customer service agent on the phone. Take care and be kind. You never know how or when that will come back to you.

Additionally, take care with your appearance. Hate me if you want for what I'm about to say, but what I'm about to share with you is based on some serious fancy-pants research.

PACKAGING

The Research

Sociological studies show that people prefer attractive, healthy-looking people over unattractive, unhealthy-looking people.[5] Research also shows that people tend to rate attractive, healthy-looking people as more successful than unattractive, unhealthy-looking people.[6]

Before you become outraged about what I just said, I think it *flat out stinks* for anyone to be judged on appearance. Appearance has nothing to do with your character or quality as a human being. Period. I wish the world worked differently, because I know that there are a lot of perfectly competent, highly talented, and skilled people in the world who get passed over and aren't treated as well as others, simply on the basis of how they look. I don't think it's morally right to prefer attractive people over unattractive people. But my beliefs don't change the fact that—like it or not—*it's just how the world works.* You can choose to ignore that fact, or you can choose to understand it and use it to your advantage.

> **You represent your brand. Every time you're out in the world and every time you speak to someone on the phone, you represent your brand.**

But know this: You *are* a part of your brand. You represent your company and the name of your business. If you think that your appearance isn't a part of that, *you're absolutely wrong.*

As I said, studies show that attractive, healthy-looking people are generally perceived to be more successful, and we know that people tend to do business with those they know, like, and trust. When you put these two things together, you can bet that the way you present yourself has something to do with how well people know, like, and trust you, and thus, your appearance *does* have an impact on whether or not people will want to do business with you.

Plus, people who take care of themselves and present themselves in a neat and tidy way are people who show that they have respect for themselves. If I think that you have respect for yourself, then I think you'll respect me and, by proxy, my business, more than someone who doesn't respect himself enough to wear a clean shirt to a meeting with me.

Making Improvements

What can you do about your appearance? First, it starts from within. Now, I can hear some of you laughing at that statement. If you're laughing it's because you don't believe it, but only because you haven't experienced it. But all you have to do is look around you to see a working example of what I'm talking about.

Often, men and women who are considered attractive are, indeed, pretty high up on the scales of what, culturally, we've defined as "perfect." But just as often, you'll see a woman who's slightly overweight or has crooked teeth who somehow magically manages to be the life of the party. You may not even have noticed that she carried a few extra pounds.

Sometimes the guy who's the most in demand isn't the most handsome. But he is the most interesting and more important, he's the most *confident.* Confidence is hugely important to how people perceive you and can actually make the things that you're insecure about *virtually invisible*.

The goal isn't to make yourself perfect. People don't care if they're doing business with a Barbie or Ken doll. The goal is to *work with what you have and make the most of it.* If you've ever watched any of those fashion makeover shows, you know that a change in their hair, clothes, and makeup can transform the way a person looks and even *stands.*

Appearance is surface stuff, even though it starts from within. But since you *can* make dramatic changes by changing easy stuff, why not do it? (And for the record, just in case you're worried, this isn't about changing your style, unless your style is "scruffy couch potato.")

So let's start with an inventory.

Conducting the Inventory

Look in the mirror and conduct an honest head-to-toe assessment of yourself. Are you tidy in your appearance? Do you take care of yourself? Are your clothes pressed and neat, or are you a wrinkled mess? Are they old and worn, or do they look clean and in good condition? Do your clothes fit well? Are your shoes scuffed or do they look new? Is your hairstyle current?

Ladies, if you wear makeup, have you checked to see if your makeup is current *and* flattering? All it takes is a trip to a makeup counter or two for an update.

When you conduct your assessment, take note of positives as well as areas where you can improve. What's your favorite feature? Start playing that up, because it's the thing you love the most about yourself. Focusing on that area will increase your confidence.

If you're not sure how you appear to others, ask a friend you trust to be honest with you. I'm not going to lie to you: It might hurt. But you can only improve if you're honest about where you are today. Find someone who can get real with you and tell you the God's honest truth about where you need to improve—not someone who will be spiteful, but a real, caring friend.

Even if I run a company called Business in Blue Jeans, you'll *never* find me in *scruffy* jeans, unless I'm working in the yard at home. If you're at home, wear whatever you want. I'm talking about what you wear when you're out in the world representing your business. If I'm at a meeting or an event or if I'm speaking (or even doing a webinar where I can be seen), I'm representing Business in Blue Jeans, so I'll wear designer jeans, an upscale top, and fabulous shoes.

There's one other thing you need to check. I can't believe I'm actually writing this, but let's face it, there's a world of aromas out there, some of them not so great. So smokers, garlic-lovers, and tree-huggers who hate deodorant, you need to know that your scent sends a powerful (sometimes *very* powerful) message. So that friend you asked to give you his or her opinion? Ask her to lean in and—yes, I'm really saying this—take a whiff. Whether it's the cigarette you enjoyed in the car or the perfume or aftershave you doused yourself before you left the house, the last thing you want to do is give someone a headache or a stomachache. Statistics show that causing potential customers and clients to be physically ill will not make a decision to buy (those statistics are totally made up, but that doesn't make them any less true).

The Business in Blue Jeans philosophy *isn't* about being lazy about your personal presentation. It's about creating a business that feels like your favorite pair of jeans: comfortable, fun, and lasting. So please don't think that if you're building a Business in Blue Jeans-style business of your own, you should just wear your old, ripped Levis. That's not the point.

Integration

Your brand should be integrated across everything you do in your business. From the moment the customer experience begins—whether that's the first glimpse of your web site or the sound of the person answering the phone or the first time seeing a poster with your logo on it—to the final "thank you for your business," and beyond, every second that a consumer is in contact with your company in *any* way should be infused with your brand.

Everyone in your company needs to know what the brand message and style is, but also what the brand voice is. They need to know it, live it, breathe it. (That means smart hiring, too, but we'll get to that in an upcoming chapter).

Some companies create a branding guide (sometimes called a "brand bible"), which tells their employees everything they need to know about the company, what it stands for, and what the "voice" of the company is. Some companies are exceptional at infusing the office workspace with their brand so that they hardly even need a branding guide.

> **Every second that a consumer is in contact with your company in any way should be infused with your brand.**

If you don't have employees or think you won't have them for quite some time, it's still a good idea to get your brand guide started and make it a work in progress. You never know—you might get so busy that you have to hire some staff. By then you'll already have the work done and can add people with minimal stress: plug and play!

Your brand name, logo, web site, marketing copywriting, products and services, and all of your marketing materials should be integrated with the brand so there's cohesion across the board. You don't want a brochure that looks completely different from your business card. You don't want a business card that doesn't match up with your web site. That just doesn't jibe. So make sure that everything works together. Otherwise your business will look like a creepy patchwork doll.

HOMEWORK ASSIGNMENT:
YOUR BRAND STYLING AND INTEGRATION

Newbies:

What is the style of your brand? List adjectives that describe your brand.

Conduct an inventory of yourself. Do you represent your business appropriately?

Existing Business Owners:

Check your brand style. Does it match up with the visual aspects of your brand?

Do you and your employees represent your brand well? Conduct a full inventory.

Is your brand integrated across your business? Do your logo, marketing materials, web site, and any other visual aspects of your brand match up?

LEANING INTO YOUR MARKETING

LEANING INTO YOUR MARKETING

You have your fire and expertise. You've figured out what your sweet spot is, you've made your way through that "workhorse phase," and have packaged that sweet spot into a brilliant, profitable business model, and you've created an amazing brand. *Now what?*

Now we're going to get to the "shout it from the mountaintops" part of business: marketing. This is where you tell people about your business and draw them in like bees to honey. But you're going to do it in a different way than everyone else does it. You're going to *lean in*.

WHAT IS MARKETING?

First, what is marketing? Marketing is anything that delivers your message to your target market. Marketing is all the ways you get your brand in front of their eyeballs.

A huge part of your business encompasses social media, web sites, newsletters (electronic and printed), blogs, direct mail, brochures, trade shows, online and offline advertising, public relations, and so, so much more…it's *all* marketing.

What you need to know about marketing is that it's *not* about blanketing the world with your message. It's not about choosing as many tactics as you can and hoping that some of them yield results.

Marketing is successful when you choose the smartest methods that reach your audience in the most effective, efficient manner and then deliver your message in a creative, interesting way that not only attracts your target market, but also engages them with your brand.

You could find thousands of strategies to market your business, but they wouldn't all be right for your unique business. The key is choosing the *right* strategies to market your business.

You know who your target market is. You know what they want. You know where to find them. And you know what your message is and how they want to hear it. Now you brainstorm creative and interesting ways to deliver that message.

It would be impossible for me to cover all the various marketing channels and ways that you can reach your target market. To do justice to that topic, I'd have to write a much, much longer book than my publisher will allow. Plus, the marketing channels you choose should be dictated by your target market. As such, you'll choose a different combination of methods to reach your target market than another reader might. Every business is unique, and you must use your research to tell you which marketing channels make the most sense for your business.

> **Marketing is successful when you choose the smartest methods that reach your audience in the most effective, efficient manner and then deliver your message in a creative, interesting way that attracts your target market and engages them with your brand.**

So instead of focusing on specific tactics, in this chapter I'm going to show you how to choose from the myriad of opportunities to market to your audience and talk about the philosophy of leaning into your marketing. I'll give you examples of how some companies are leaning into their marketing as well as examples of a few companies that are decidedly leaning *away* from their marketing so that you can see how it works and get some ideas for how to put this into practice in your own business. That way, you can create a marketing plan that encompasses leaning in within each of your chosen marketing channels.

Creating a Marketing Plan

Since we're well over halfway through this book and I haven't even mentioned business plans, you've probably figured out that I'm not a fan of business plans for most situations (except in cases where you're seeking funding; then you pretty much have to have one). In my experience, most aspiring entrepreneurs spend absurd amounts of time and energy on overly formal, stuffy, structured business plans, only to toss them in a drawer later and never look at them again. What a waste of time, effort, and paper!

Maybe it's that I usually have an overarching business plan of some type in my head, or maybe it's that I've seen too many people who found the idea of a structured business plan so daunting that they just never realized their dreams, but I just don't see why anyone would have to have one of these things.

I've heard some businesspeople say that if you can't write a business plan, you have no hopes of being a successful business owner. That's such a bunch of hogwash that I can't even find a bucket big enough for it. The people who say this nonsense are usually wearing extremely uncomfortable-looking suits and ties that are clearly tied too tight. The oxygen just isn't getting to their brains.

Many successful entrepreneurs I know today have *never* written a business plan. In fact, many of them would tell you that they haven't written a marketing plan, either. While you don't need a business *or* marketing plan in the sense of a formal document that's written to someone else's specifications, what you *do* need is a *plan*.

And sure, your plan *can* be one of those weighty, overly formal documents, but your plan can just as easily be something you wrote down on a paper napkin or drew up on a whiteboard in your office.

This book is about running a business in *your own style, on your own terms,* and there's no reason why you have to follow anyone else's rules. For some people, business and marketing plans help to organize thoughts and structure the business. Other people don't need to write it down. Still others find a flowchart to be just as useful.

Do what works best for you. Conceptualize how you're going to reach your target market and which channels you're going to use, and map it out. It doesn't have to be complicated.

HOMEWORK ASSIGNMENT:
CHOOSING YOUR INITIAL MARKETING CHANNELS

Newbies and Existing Business Owners:

Revisit the homework assignments where you got to know your target market.

Start making a list of places where you can find your target market. This list should include blogs, magazines, newspapers, web sites, stores, radio shows (online and offline), television shows, and products they use and companies they like.

Look at your list and consider how you can connect with your target market.

Can you partner with other companies your target market does business with?

Can you send your product to blogs they read?

Can you advertise in or be interviewed for one of the media outlets (magazines, newspapers, radio shows, and so on) they connect with?

Are there other ways to reach your target market?

Can you capture their contact details and send them an e-mail or printed newsletter?

Are they interested in learning via teleseminars or webinars? Make a list of things you could teach them.

Are they interested in learning via video? Make a list of videos you could shoot.

Once you've chosen a few channels that could work for your business, then you can apply the philosophy of leaning into your marketing to each channel.

LEANING IN: THE PHILOSOPHY

Have you ever had a fantastic conversation with someone where you were so interested in what the other person had to say that you were leaning in so far that you were practically falling out of your seat? That's the essence of the philosophy of leaning into your marketing.

Leaning in is a physical expression, a body gesture that tells people you care about what they have to say. When you lean into your marketing, you tell your target market you care what *they* have to say; more importantly, you're willing to act on it.

> **When you lean into your marketing, you tell your target market you care what they have to say; more importantly, you're willing to act on it.**

Back in the old days, companies didn't have to interact with their customers, at least not the way we do today. Companies had customer service phone lines where you'd call for help, and that was about it. When I was growing up, long customer service lines were a favorite topic in the Sunday comic strips.

Today, everything's different. Customers with concerns head to social media and into the blogosphere to make their cases in the public eye. Companies can't hide behind sterile customer service departments. And with companies like Zappos striving to create a world-class customer experience, businesses can't afford to ignore the customer experience. In fact, leaning into your marketing is a philosophy that combines marketing with the customer experience, because customer experience has become so vital to a company's success.

Leaning into your marketing means engaging with your customers in your marketing and delivering an incredible experience. It's making your research about your target market and your desire to understand them continuous and ongoing *and* engaging in every step of the process with them to ensure they have an amazing experience.

This engagement takes place in *every* facet of your business, and the method entails *you* going to *them* and going a step beyond. Your marketing is where the conversation begins. The *leaning in* is the part where the engagement goes that extra step beyond.

THE BIG MISTAKES IN MARKETING

Broadcasting

The goal of marketing isn't to just promote, promote, promote. If all you're doing is broadcasting your message, you're just advertising, like a giant billboard looking down on the world and telling everyone what to buy, in the hopes that someone will respond.

Do you know which commercials and ads are the most successful? They're the ones that make us feel and the ones that make us think. Most commercials just broadcast the message. They leave us bored or cold. Either way, we're not engaged.

When you're laughing, crying, or feeling *something*, or when you're thinking about the commercial later, you've become engaged. That's why shock advertisements like the ones I discussed earlier work. They're so intense that you can't help but become engaged by them.

Some marketing mediums are specifically designed to be engaging. Social media, for example, is meant to be social. It's a tool, a mechanism that allows us to transform the in-person experience into a continuous online experience. When you post in social media, your goal is to engage and create dialogue. Inspire people into discussion. Engender debate. Further the conversation in your industry.

Tostitos

Tostitos is a great example of a brand that broadcasts in social media. All it takes is a quick glance through their Twitter feed to see that they don't interact with their following of over 15,000. There are no retweets, no replies, there is literally no interaction at all.

It's not like there are no opportunities for them to interact and engage, either. In just a few days, I counted fifteen opportunities they missed to communicate with followers who had directly commented to them, including Pepsi!

When you broadcast and don't interact with your following, you miss the opportunity to share your brand but also to connect people to it.

You miss the opportunity to create a loyal fan base that cares about your company.

Ignoring Your Audience

In previous eras, marketing was simpler for companies because they could ignore the audience. Ignoring the audience was convenient for advertisers and marketers because it provided them with the illusion that they were controlling the message and the brand experience. Problem is, you can't control what goes on at the water cooler. You can't control what goes on in your target market's minds.

One of the biggest mistakes I see in social media is when companies tweet or post about deals and how cool their product or their web site is, but they ignore what their customers are saying *to* them. They simply don't respond.

American Airlines vs United Airlines

Recently, my husband and I were traveling to England, and when one of our flights was delayed and we were about to miss a connecting flight, American Airlines booked us on a United flight to get us to our final destination on time. Our bags remained on the American Airlines flight.

From the airport, because I was frustrated with American, I headed to social media and tweeted to United Airlines that this was a great opportunity for them to earn my business. United didn't respond, but American sure did: "Susan! Don't cheat on us!" they laughingly tweeted.

Then American Airlines engaged me in a full conversation on Twitter about what happened with my flight. They located my bags and told me they'd make sure they got to the UK. It didn't *quite* work out as well as I'd hoped—I had to tweet every day to ask them to check on my bags (what a *much* better story this would be if they had just kept tabs on everything for me), but they faithfully responded and my bags did arrive safe and sound, albeit two days late.

Still, don't tell me that when, on our flights home, American bumped us up to Business Class, it was *just* because of our Platinum status with the airline. I'm guessing somebody put a note on my record.

> **You can't ignore your audience anymore. If you do, you're handing your target market to anyone else who offers the same service, but is willing to engage and lean in.**

In sharp contrast, United never responded. Not a peep, not a word. The service on their flight was fine, but I'll take being valued and receiving fantastic customer service over being ignored any day of the week.

You can't ignore your audience anymore. If you do, you're handing your target market to anyone else who offers the same service, but is willing to engage and lean in. It's just that simple.

THE KEYS TO LEANING INTO YOUR MARKETING

Targeting

"Sometimes more isn't better, Linus. Sometimes it's just more."
—Sabrina, in the movie *Sabrina*

You don't have to be in every marketing medium. In fact, you *shouldn't* be in every marketing channel, because your audience won't be everywhere. You shouldn't try to get on every talk show. You shouldn't send your product to every blogger. You shouldn't try to be on every social media site. You shouldn't try to advertise in every single magazine and newspaper.

Being in every marketing channel doesn't make you better or get you more business. It just means you're spending more money and have more work to do to keep up.

Instead of spreading yourself too thin, find out where your target market spends their time and go where they are. Devote yourself to the marketing channels where you'll get the strongest response and the biggest bang for your buck.

Cartier

Cartier is one of the world's leading luxury jewelry companies. In 2009 and 2010, Cartier tweeted twenty-five times in total. With over 18,000 followers, you'd think they would've tweeted more, but also that they'd still be tweeting, right? Wrong.

In 2010, Cartier abruptly (or so it seemed to the rest of the world) abandoned Twitter entirely and invested their time and energy into Facebook, where they have over 191,000 fans.

> " Instead of spreading yourself too thin, devote yourself to the marketing channels where you'll get the strongest response and the biggest "bang for your buck." "

Could Cartier have built a stronger following in the Twittersphere had they stayed? Undoubtedly. But the question of numbers isn't nearly as important as the question of whether they would've been reaching the right demographic, their target market. Cartier made a clear, calculated decision to focus their efforts on Facebook, where they thought their target market would be better reached.

As you analyze what you know about your target market, make sure you know where you'll find them. This is a huge part of making the most of your time—why put effort and energy into a platform that won't yield results? This is the kind of thinking you should put into *every* marketing strategy.

HOMEWORK ASSIGNMENT:
TARGETING

Newbies:

Where will you find your target market? Online? Offline?
What's the most effective way to reach them in these places?

Existing Business Owners:

How do you currently reach your audience?
Are you reaching them where they are most readily found?

> List out the marketing strategies you're currently using and assess
> their effectiveness.
>
> Which strategies bring in the bulk of your buyers? How can you
> beef up those strategies?

Engagement

Marketing is all about engagement in today's world. It's connecting with your audience and talking *to* them, soliciting feedback, and leaning in by continuing to engage and deliver again and again and again.

Leaning into your marketing isn't just *talking* to your target market, though. It goes well beyond that to forming relationships with your customers and building on those relationships. Here are some examples to show you how some companies are (and aren't) leaning into their marketing:

Guayaki

My husband is from Uruguay, where the tea-like drink yerba mate (pronounced "ZHER-ba MAH-tay") is a cultural custom and part of the lifestyle. The boost you get from drinking yerba mate is better than what you get from soda or coffee, and it's healthier for you, too. Since we fell in love, I've been drinking mate, and when I'm home, I favor Guayaki, a brand that brings yerba mate to the United States in various forms. I've mentioned how much I enjoy their products on Twitter many times.

In fact, Guayaki initiated a conversation with me on Twitter because I was talking about yerba mate. I wasn't talking about their company, but mentioned the words *yerba mate*. Guayaki was tracking *yerba mate* as a keyword (you can set up various social media tools to track certain keywords so that you can respond to them).

They initiated the conversation with me as a potential member of their target market. They *engaged* with me. When they saw I was looking for a way to stay awake for my thirty-six-hour-long Guinness World Records® event, they leaned into their marketing by sponsoring my event and sending me a case of yerba mate drinks for the event.

When you see people talking about your business, brand, area of expertise, or industry, get involved with them. Ask them questions, give them feedback, or just send them a "thumbs up." That's what engagement is all about.

Once you have the conversation going, take it further and lean into the marketing. How can you take it one step beyond?

Crutchfield

Last Christmas, Leo and I decided to upgrade our home theater system. We called a local company to give us a quote on the purchase and installation of what we were after and told the salesman how much we wanted to spend and what features were important to us. He came to the house, took notes and measurements, and said he'd send us a quote. When he e-mailed me the quote, it was almost twice what we had decided to spend, so we reminded him of the budget we'd given him, but he wouldn't budge.

Leo and I did some research and discovered that the company that makes the high-end components from the quote also makes the same exact components with a consumer label on them. These components sell for substantially less money, and they were available at Crutchfield.

Crutchfield sells audio and video equipment and electronics, but they're not like any other company in this market. Crutchfield is one of the most engaged companies I've encountered.

When I called Crutchfield, the salesman was *incredible*. He took his time, asked me questions, gave me options, made suggestions, and when all was said and done, we came in *under* budget. He told me that when the items arrived, I could call back and someone would walk me through installing everything.

Our items arrived quickly, everything was exactly as we expected, and indeed, when we called in, the tech guys walked me through the installation, including the installation of a part we didn't buy from them. The original salesman even e-mailed me to make sure everything was OK.

Eight months later, our remote control started acting funny. I called Crutchfield, and they sent us a new one with a box and a label to send the old one back to them. They made everything easy.

The Crutchfield web site featured a picture of Bill Crutchfield, the founder and CEO. Next to Bill's photo, the text reads, "Because my name is on the business, I work hard to make sure you get the best possible shopping experience. I look forward to hearing your comments."

If Crutchfield wanted to lean into their marketing any further, they'd probably fall over.

Krystal vs. White Castle

Recently, I was involved in a fairly silly Twitter discussion with two friends, John Michael Morgan and Chris Reimer, in which we were debating the merits of Krystal versus White Castle.

Suddenly, even though we hadn't included anyone else in the conversation but the three of us, White Castle tweeted a link to a photo...in which they had Photoshopped a picture of Chris, who'd been defending White Castle's honor, into a White Castle ad, as if he'd just photobombed the ad. (Want to see the photo? Visit the book site at http://BusinessInBlueJeans. com/book.) It was *awesome*.

Just as Guayaki was watching out for people talking about *yerba mate*, White Castle was looking for people talking about *White Castle*. Because they saw the conversation, they were able to jump in to create a personalized *experience*.

After White Castle posted the photo, John tweeted, "This actually makes me like White Castle a bit more. I don't hear Krystal chiming in! LOL" Chris and I agreed and encouraged Krystal to participate.

Krystal was silent until the next day—which presents me with a great opportunity to tell you that in social media, *speed matters*. White Castle got a leg up on Krystal simply by responding fastest.

When Krystal joined the conversation, they tweeted photos...of their food—nothing like the personalized image that White Castle had created. Later, they posted another image of a superhero hot dog, saying, "We're here to help you, @johnmorgan! Sending in reinforcements." It was cute, but certainly not the kind of engagement that we'd gotten from White Castle.

The conversation and friendly rivalry continued, and Krystal and White Castle followed each of us, which is cool in the Twittersphere. What's interesting about this scenario is that both companies were *engaged*, albeit at different levels and in different ways.

Most of this engagement continued *after* I mentioned that I don't eat meat and I don't even have a Krystal located in my state! Suddenly, these two companies that I never think about are now on my radar. I might not eat meat (often), but my husband eats burgers. After the fun we had online, he had his first White Castle experience that very night.

HOMEWORK ASSIGNMENT:
ENGAGEMENT

Newbies:

What are some ways you can engage with your target market?

Existing Business Owners:

Do you currently engage with your target market?
How can you improve your engagement?

Consistency

Marketing requires consistency. You can't expect a single act of marketing (say, one blog post) to change the life of your business. Marketing is an ongoing, never-ending process that you should always be engaged in so that you have a continuing flow of business coming through your doors.

If you haven't posted in your blog in over a month, you've lost readers. If you missed a month or two sending out your newsletter (electronic or printed), they'll be surprised when they receive the next one. If you don't know when you last updated your social media status, the world of social media has probably forgotten about you. That's how it goes. Time passes faster in social media than it does in the rest of the world. So if you haven't posted something in three months, that's like three years in social media time.

> **Marketing is an ongoing, never-ending process that requires consistency.**

J.Crew

J.Crew, a popular clothing company, used to be active on Twitter. But they disappeared one day, quite abruptly, similar to Cartier. Unlike Cartier, however, J.Crew still links to their Twitter profile from their main web site, giving the impression that they still want you to follow them. In fact, they're still mentioned frequently by people on Twitter, which makes me think they should still maintain an active presence there.

If you were to delve into J.Crew's older tweets, though, you'd see that even when they were actively tweeting, it wasn't with regularity. They'd tweet maybe once a week, if that. Once a week isn't enough participation on Twitter, which moves at such a rapid pace that anything less than a once-a-day check-in is doing the platform a huge disservice.

You can't let social media profiles languish. They're not intended to be static web sites. They're designed to be living, breathing representations of you in the online world. If you don't update them regularly, people will wonder if you're dead. And quite possibly, you will be, at least online, for all intents and purposes.

Also, it's rarely a good idea to adopt a start-and-stop methodology to your marketing strategies. Instead, employ a regular, consistent plan that you can manage effectively. If you find that it's too difficult to manage everything, then cut back to the strategies that bring you the most business and devote your time and attention to them.

HOMEWORK ASSIGNMENT:
CONSISTENCY

Newbies:

Now that you've figured out who your target market is and identified some ways that you can reach them and places where you can engage with them, look at your list and decide if it will be possible for you to keep up with everything on the list. If it seems like too much, narrow the list down to what seems like the most important elements. Keep narrowing until you have a list that seems like something you can manage regularly and reliably.

Existing Business Owners:

Analyze your existing marketing plan. Is it easily managed? If not, which strategies are bringing in the most business? Narrow it down to just those strategies so that your plan is more manageable and consistent.

Educating Your Target Market

Many entrepreneurs are aware of the power of educating their target market. As business owners in today's marketplace, we're not just selling products and services, but acting as a resource—to our target market, to the media, to everyone.

I don't just consult with my clients, I also write educational blog articles, speak in public to all kinds of audiences, hold educational teleseminars and webinars, and a great deal of other things, all in the interest of educating people about why business rocks, simple things you can do to improve your business, and the state of business today.

Articles and Blogging

Writing articles and blogging are easy ways to become a resource, be seen as an expert, and market your business at the same time. Write articles that relate to your industry and that will be of interest to your target market, and then post the articles in your blog, on others' blogs, on relevant sites where your target market will be, or send in a pitch to pertinent magazines that accept freelance work.

> **As business owners in today's marketplace, we're not just selling products and services, but acting as a resource.**

Pay attention to the quality of your writing, especially if you're submitting your work to other outlets. While there are no official rules with blogging, there's no substitute for clean, clear writing.

One of my clients hates writing. We knew she would never be an avid blogger if she had to write all the time. She *loves* speaking, so instead of a written blog she has a video blog. She records videos and posts them to YouTube, then embeds the YouTube videos into her blog, instead of written articles. It's worked out beautifully. Whether you record videos or write articles, either is an effective strategy because your web site becomes a living, breathing resource for your target market.

Red Letter Paper Company

Red Letter Paper Company is one of my favorite clients. A Christian greeting company that was founded when CEO Stephanie Hinderer couldn't find a greeting card that delivered a Christian sentiment without looking like something her grandmother would send, they offer a wide range of really cool, modern-looking designs.

But Stephanie doesn't just make and sell greeting cards. She also writes blog articles for her company web site about the value of sending a tangible paper greeting card, about the right way to write a thank-you note, how to improve your handwriting, and about all kinds of things around the greeting card and gift industry.

She's not just a provider of a commodity. She's a resource.

Crutchfield

Remember that story about Crutchfield and my home theater? Before I called them to place my order, I studied Crutchfield's web site, because they have an enormous amount of information there. They've posted articles on choosing the right systems for your home, videos on installation, and anything else you could possibly need to outfit yourself with the right electronics.

They've taken the concept of educating the consumer to a new level. Crutchfield is a *resource* and not just a retailer, simply by educating their target market.

Other Ways to Educate

There are many ways to educate your target market and become a resource while marketing your business.

Impress Rubber Stamps

Impress Stamps is a Washington-based company that sells rubber stamps and greeting card-making supplies. Every season they create dozens of card designs and post them on their web site, along with a list of all the supplies used to make each card.

By educating their target market about what can be done with the supplies they sell, their stamps and supplies sell *far* better than if they'd just posted pictures of the stamps on their web site.

Additionally, they have classes at all of their locations, so that their customers can come in and learn in person, alongside others who are interested in similar crafts and hobbies.

HOMEWORK ASSIGNMENT:
EDUCATING YOUR TARGET MARKET

Newbies:

How could you educate your target market?

Make a list of options to educate your target market.

Add these elements to your marketing plan. Remember, only include the things that are the most important and keep it manageable!

Existing Business Owners:

Do you currently educate your target market?

What are some methods that you could add that would educate your target market?

MARKETING WITH CONSCIENCE

Another fundamental principle of leaning into your marketing is to market with conscience. Marketing with conscience is, essentially, finding a way to do some good in the world with your business.

For example, I donate a percentage of the profits from my consulting company to charitable causes that I've chosen as my personal "pet" projects. I list them on my web site so that others can become more aware of the charities I support and might choose to donate to them, too. I also offer a discount off of my regular fees to veterans.

Marketing with conscience is doing good for the world and giving back to the community that supports and sustains your business. There are many ways to engage in marketing with conscience, but the goal is to lean into your community the same way you lean into your target market.

And, to paraphrase my friends Bob Burg and John David Mann, co-authors of *The Go-Giver*, this is a great way to show up in the world...and it's highly profitable. There's nothing wrong with that. In fact, in *The Go-Giver*, Bob and John say that "the key to effective giving is to stay open to receiving." Essentially, receiving balances giving.

Imagine a cup filled with water. Pour the water from that cup, a little each into several other cups. When you're done, your original cup is empty. But if you have a way to refill that cup, you can keep pouring water into the other cups until they're full. Giving is amazing, but receiving allows you to give *even more*. That's why marketing with conscience can help you and your business to change the world.

> "Marketing with conscience is finding a way to do some good in the world with your business."

There are tons of ways to market with conscience, and of course, as always, your job is to get creative and find the best ways to reach your target market *and* market with conscience.

The Container Store

Companies often reach out to the local community, but The Container Store does it best. Whenever a new store opens, The Container Store looks at the non-profits in the area and finds one that is largely supported by The Container Store's target market. The Container Store then donates a percentage of sales from opening weekend of their new store to that non-profit. The supporters of the non-profit, who are in The Container Store's target market, then become customers of the new store *and* a volunteer marketing force to get the word out about the store.

The Container Store also gives donations and gift cards to community events, fundraisers, and auctions, as well as donating organization makeovers for non-profit facilities, and facilitating company-sponsored volunteer opportunities.

Whole Foods

Whole Foods embraces the concept of "conscious capitalism" by allowing each store to decide how it can best contribute to the local community. Since stores are staffed by locals, they know the community best. They also automatically donate food to local area food pantries, encourage volunteer work among employees, and hold five percent days, where five percent of net sales from the store on that day is donated to a local non-profit.

Whole Foods also supports foundations that encourage improvement of children's nutrition and help the poor in developing world countries through micro-loans for entrepreneurship and support for community projects.

When to Market With Conscience

Marketing with conscience means learning how to market and grow your company while also doing good in the world. It's giving back to the community that supports you.

Before you start giving away a percentage of your business to charity, let me say that fledgling businesses shouldn't reasonably donate a percentage of revenue until they're solvent and profitable.

However, as you can see from these examples, there are *many* ways that you can market with conscience that don't require you to give away your profits until you realistically can do so without hurting the business and its growth. Volunteer your time. If you're a service provider, dedicate a certain number of hours each month for pro bono work. Find ways to partner with non-profits. Get creative and lean into your community.

HOMEWORK ASSIGNMENT:
MARKETING WITH CONSCIENCE

Newbies and Existing Business Owners:

Begin to make a list of non-profit companies that have the same target market as you do.

Are there ways that you could partner with these companies or contribute to them?

What are some ways for you to lean into your local community?

EXTRAORDINARY CUSTOMER EXPERIENCES

Extraordinary customer experiences are the icing on the cake of leaning into your marketing. Most commonly, we think of customer service as a separate entity from marketing and everything else in the business—something that's "after the fact." But customer service is still a part of your marketing plan.

Want repeat sales? Want your customers to be delighted with their choice to buy from you? Deliver extraordinary customer service. Give your clientele the best experience they've ever had and they'll become loyal to you forever.

How to Create an Extraordinary Customer Experience

Extraordinary customer experiences don't happen by accident. They happen by design. You can create an extraordinary experience for your clients by examining every single moment that you have an opportunity to reach your target market and finding ways to go one, two, or several steps beyond the norm.

Engaged, Empowered Employees

Who's most important to your company?

I'll bet you said "customers" or "clients." Wrong answer.

Your employees come first. *Then* your customers. Choose your employees wisely (and this includes virtual employees), and invest in them with the best training, and you'll have a company that's worth its weight in gold. Your employees *are* your company.

If your employees are less than thrilled with their jobs and what they do and with how you handle things, and if they're rarely rewarded, then they'll be unsatisfied and unfulfilled. Their lack of fulfillment will get translated to your customers. When customers see unhappy employees, they become uneasy and uncomfortable.

Michael's

When I received my title certificate from Guinness World Records®, I naturally wanted to have it framed. I'd had other things framed at Michael's craft store and they'd done good work. The last time I had something framed there, I had a stellar experience with a staff member who clearly loved what she did and was excited to help me. I found her so helpful when I was choosing mat colors and frames during that visit, in fact, that Michael's was the only place I considered for this important job.

Unfortunately, this visit was completely different. While the staff members were impressed that I had achieved a Guinness World Records® title, they weren't helpful with framing recommendations.

When I went to pick up the framed certificate two weeks later, the framer had sliced too far into a corner of the mat. I said, "Oh, I'm so disappointed. There's a cut in the corner of the mat." The sales associate was so disengaged he didn't even respond. I pointed to the mat and repeated myself, and he leaned over, looked at the mat and said, "It's done by machine. Sometimes that happens," and looked away.

> **❝ Your employees come first. Then your customers. ❞**

I pressed the issue, and the guy said it would take another two weeks to re-do the framing. Not only was there no way for him to get it done faster, but there was no way to be sure that I would be any happier with the results. I still sent the certificate back, but walked away disappointed—more with how detached this guy was from my experience than with having to send my certificate back for two more weeks.

For the record, when I went back two weeks later, the new mat was also cut, though slightly less than the previous one. The same employee helped me, and he cared just as little as before, so much so, in fact, that my husband (who's more patient than I am) commented on it.

Hiring

The most important way to create an empowered, engaged staff is to hire well. Zappos, for example, conducts two interviews with new hires: one with the department where the applicant will be working, to ensure that the applicant has the necessary skills for the position, and one with the human resources department, to ensure that the person will fit into the corporate culture. Similarly, Danny Meyer, founder of Union Square Hospitality Group, owner of many restaurants in New York and the author of *Setting the Table,* puts heavy emphasis on ensuring that all employees are team players who will support and respect each other, and on encouraging a sense of team spirit in the corporate culture.

When you hire people who can do their job well *and* form a strong, supportive team, you create a workforce that is prepared to serve your customers and clients impeccably and happily.

Compensation

The guy who "helped" me at Michael's that day was a sales associate, which is not a highly paid position. That was part of the problem. Employees who aren't paid well in comparison to other, similar positions and who aren't rewarded or appreciated in other ways tend to be dissatisfied and to see their jobs as a way to pay the bills. They tend *not* to be invested in how well they do their jobs.

On the other hand, when employees are paid well, compensated in a variety of ways, and shown appreciation for their efforts, they tend to perform well in their jobs and to care about the results they get for their customers *and* for the company.

Elite SEM

Elite SEM, a search engine marketing company, is widely considered one of the best places to work. It's consistently rated highly by employees and customers. Elite SEM has some fascinating means of rewarding employees.

> **When you hire people who can do their job well and form a strong, supportive team, you create a workforce that is prepared to serve your customers and clients impeccably and happily.**

Employees of Elite SEM receive unlimited vacation and sick days. You'd think no one would work, right? But in fact, they have a lot of rewards and compensations that make people *want* to work. A vast percentage of the profit from client work goes to the employees. The more they work, the more they can make. Plus, because of the digital nature of the company's service, employees can work from home or take a working vacation overseas.

Every quarter, employees vote for one employee who has gone the extra mile. The company gives the person with the most votes a free, weeklong vacation, including plane tickets, lodging, and spending money.

Finally, Elite SEM provides each employee with free meals before, during, and after their workdays and a learning budget to spend on seminars, courses, workshops, and training to stay current on technology.

All of this effort to build an employee-centric corporate culture pays off. Elite SEM has had *zero turnover* in its eight years (as of the writing of this book, literally *no one* has ever quit). Their clients are delighted with the results of the service they've received.

Obviously, Elite SEM provides a digital service that makes flexible work possible, but even if your industry isn't as flexible, there are ways to improve your compensation plans with "bonus benefits" like learning budgets, meals, employee recognition, and fun things like game rooms. Just remember that in this part of your business, your target market is your employees, so find out what *they* want and what will make the difference to them. A pool table might seem like something your employees might enjoy during breaks, but if it's not what they want, it'll sit unused, an ever-present reminder of misunderstanding your workforce.

Freedom (Empowerment)

Going back to my bad framing experience, how great would it have been if, instead of being totally disengaged from my experience, the sales associate had said something like, "I see the problem. I'm so sorry this happened. This piece is clearly important to you, and I want you to be happy every time you look at it hanging on your wall. Let me see how quickly I can get this fixed for you."

What if this employee actually had been free to *do* something about my dissatisfaction? Too often, employees simply don't have the power to fix things. Companies are set up so managers or customer service agents handle problems or mistakes. This structure creates a culture of "passing the buck."

Got a problem with a product? Call customer service. Someone else will handle that. Got a problem with your order? We have a *department* for that. Too often, customer service and handling mistakes are handled by a department, which means everybody is so busy passing the buck to the next guy that nobody thinks about what the customer is experiencing *or* takes responsibility for it.

Freeing your employees means removing restrictions that prevent them from handling problems that come up. It means letting them take ownership of preventing or solving problems. It means that, even if this isn't their job or their department, they're going to stay by that customer's side and make sure that something gets done so that when that customer walks away, she's shaking her head in wonder at the amazing service she's received.

Going back to the example of Michael's, if this sales associate had been freer to help, he might have been more engaged with his job. But he knew he couldn't do anything to help me. He knew he couldn't rush the job, even though it meant I would be unhappy. If he'd had the power to put a rush on the project, he would've felt more interested in helping me *because he could*. He might have been more enthusiastic about his job, because the company trusted him to do more.

Employee freedom is about more than just customer service. It's a subject that goes far deeper and is worthy of its own book. When you give your staff the freedom to do their jobs more effectively, efficiently, and usefully, and to solve challenges or problems they discover, they become more engaged and involved in what they do. They feel respected and want to live up to the trust they've been given. More importantly, when your employees know that you're leaning into them, they'll lean back.

Engaged CEOs and Executives

It's not just the employees who need to be involved and engaged. Empowerment and involvement are important at every level.

In the television show called *Undercover Boss,* CEOs and company owners don disguises to visit factory floors and retail stores within their corporations to find out what's really going on. In every episode, the CEOs are shocked to discover disgruntled workers, problems on the assembly line, and stores that aren't getting taken care of.

The sad thing about *Undercover Boss* is that it reveals a phenomenon that I've seen too many times in corporations: The boss who doesn't visit the ground floor regularly is ignorant of what's really happening in his or her company.

Costco

Jim Sinegal, one of the founders of Costco, the fifth largest retailer in the United States (as of the writing of this book), is well-known to his employees. His philosophy of running the company when he founded it was the same when he retired in January 2012: "We're going to be a company that's on a first-name basis with everyone." One of the reasons that Jim was able to remain on a first-name basis with everyone was that he regularly toured every single one of his stores, traveling more than 280 days a year.

> **The boss who doesn't visit the ground floor regularly is ignorant of what's really happening in his or her company.**

Jim knew exactly what was going on with his business. He could see when policies or changes weren't working, instead of relying on reports from people whose self-interests might get in the way of honesty. Most importantly, Jim leaned into his workforce on the ground floor, so they knew he wanted to hear what they had to say.

As the owner of your company, you need to know what's going on at all levels, even if it's a small company. No matter how many employees you have, taking the time to visit the ground floor and communicate with every level is critical to keeping your staff satisfied and productive.

Elysian Hotel

In 2011, my husband and I stayed in the Elysian Hotel in downtown Chicago. Hands down, Elysian delivered the best service I've ever experienced.

Though Leo and I had never stayed in their hotel before, every member of the hotel staff knew and remembered our names from the moment we checked in, and whenever we encountered a new member of the staff, he or she would introduce himself or herself to us. One evening, the concierge recommended a restaurant to us. The next morning, he made a point of stopping us in the lobby to ask if we had enjoyed the restaurant.

Our room was perfect, down to the smallest details. We went out shopping in the afternoon and returned to find our fireplace lit and robes and correctly-sized slippers laid out for each of us.

The hotel had black BMWs with drivers available to drive guests around the city, so one night Leo and I decided to have one of the drivers take us to Giordano's for pizza. Upon arriving at the restaurant, we discovered a massive line. The driver said, "I know of another Giordano's that's nearby, and they won't have a line. Would you like to go there instead?"

As the driver took us to the next restaurant, Leo and I talked about how much we were enjoying the hotel. I noticed that at stoplights, the driver would make notes on a small notepad. Finally, I became too curious. I asked him what he was writing.

The driver apologized and explained that while he tried not to eavesdrop on the conversations that hotel guests had in the car, the hotel manager had asked him to pay attention and take notes whenever he heard feedback about the hotel, good or bad, so the manager could reward his staff or fix any problems. That was the manager's way of "visiting the ground floor."

From check-in to checkout, this hotel is on top of their guests' entire experience. Nothing gets missed. They lean in the entire time you are their guest.

Can you imagine delivering that kind of service? Can you imagine *receiving* that kind of service? It's exactly that level of exceptional, remarkable care and attention to detail that makes your business memorable and, ultimately, lasting.

HOMEWORK ASSIGNMENT:
ENGAGED, EMPOWERED EMPLOYEES AND CEOS

Newbies:

Begin to craft a description of the corporate culture you'd like to see your company embody.

When it's time to hire staff, what are some ways that you can attract people who fit the spirit you've described?

How can you compensate your employees and what are some "bonus benefits" that you can offer them?

What are some ways that you can free your employees to solve problems and handle challenges?

How can you be an engaged CEO?

Existing Business Owners:

Describe your corporate culture.

Is your corporate culture one that attracts the best talent and prospective employees who fit into your culture?

What improvements can be made to your compensation structure? Can you add "bonus benefits" that will help your employees to feel more appreciated and rewarded?

What are some changes that you can make to improve your corporate culture so that your employees are freer to solve problems and handle challenges?

How can you be a more engaged, involved CEO?

Anticipation

Once you've hired a great team, your next task in designing an extraordinary customer experience is to anticipate every moment that you'll be able to touch your customers, even from before they make a purchase. You won't be able to capture *every* single "touchpoint" with your customers, but you can affect many of them.

Where do they first interact with your company? Is it on the web, by phone, or walking into a store? How can you make that first moment of contact a singular, special, extraordinary experience?

> **Sometimes creating an extraordinary experience is as simple as making the experience more human.**

Sometimes creating an extraordinary experience is as simple as making the experience more human. One of the reasons I love my web hosting company, Bluehost, is because I know that every time I call the company, an actual person in Utah will answer the phone. No phone trees, no "Press 1 for sales," but an actual, live, warm human being. More importantly, everyone I talk to at Bluehost takes ownership to make sure my questions get answers and my problems get solved.

HOMEWORK ASSIGNMENT:
ANTICIPATION

Newbies:

Create a map of how clients will interact with your business, from the first moment they come into contact with your business. Follow the process all the way through, designing an extraordinary customer experience.

What are some ways you can create a company that excels in designing the customer experience?

Existing Business Owners:

Map out your customer or client experience from start to finish.

Where do your clients and customers first encounter your business? Can you improve that encounter and create a better customer experience? Are there ways to maximize each point of contact to design an extraordinary customer experience?

Standing in Their Shoes

One of the best ways to create extraordinary customer experiences is to stand in the shoes of your customers and clients. Put yourself in their shoes and ask yourself, "What would I feel if I was in this position?"

If you're already in business, become your own secret shopper and experience every moment in your business. Take note of each and every detail that you notice and find ways to improve.

Marriott Manchester Airport Hotel

On our way home from enjoying the English countryside last summer, my husband and I spent a night at the Marriott Manchester Airport Hotel. When we arrived in Manchester, we were worn out from a long train ride, so we used the airport shuttle phone to call the hotel to have their shuttle pick us up.

The front desk clerk informed us that they no longer offered the shuttle service, but the hotel had made arrangements with a local cab company to bring people to the hotel...for £6. When we arrived at the hotel in our cab, a big shuttle with the name of the hotel emblazoned across the side was sitting in front of the hotel. How frustrating! They had a shuttle *sitting right there*.

We went inside and checked in and were given a map to our room. Now, it's not entirely uncommon in the United Kingdom for a hotel to have long, confusing, circuitous routes to the rooms, but this one took us as far from the front desk and civilization as you could get and ended in the basement. When we finally arrived at our room, an empty beer glass sat on the floor outside our door.

Inside the room, we discovered peeling wallpaper and a non-functioning air conditioning. A fan in the room gave away the fact that someone must have known the air conditioning wasn't working. We ordered fish and chips via room service and everything had the dark look of having been cooked in oil that hadn't been changed in months. We couldn't even bring ourselves to eat it.

Finally, fed up, I complained to the on-duty manager, who apologized profusely and offered to refund the cost of our dinner and our room. But by then, it was too late. There's nothing they could've done to get things back on track by that point. We'll never stay there again.

If one person at that hotel had walked into that room before we arrived and said to themselves, "What would I feel like if I was staying in this room?" or ordered room service and examined the food, I have a feeling we never would've experienced all the problems that we did during our stay there.

When you fail to stand in your customers' shoes, you fail to see your business through their eyes. You miss details. In the hospitality industry, especially, standing in your guests' shoes is paramount. You can't deliver an extraordinary experience unless you pay attention to the details that your guests will pay attention to. It's as simple as that.

HOMEWORK ASSIGNMENT:
STANDING IN THEIR SHOES

Newbies:

Go through your customer experience, standing in your target market's shoes. What will they experience? What do you want them to experience? Try to identify what details they'll notice and then work to create extraordinary experiences.

Existing Business Owners:

Are you currently employing any strategies to stand in your customers or clients' shoes? How can you become more aware of and enhance the details that your clients and customers notice?

Overdelivering

The essence of delivering extraordinary customer experiences is overdelivering. In my time in corporate America, I heard over and over that you should always underpromise. That way, it always seems like you're overdelivering. Sometimes it seems like the corporate world is focused on giving only the bare minimum while simultaneously maximizing profit.

That's the prevailing wisdom: The more you can minimize expenses, the more profit you make. Unfortunately, that "wisdom" is *wrong*, especially when you cut expenses by cutting service. When you cut service, you tell your customers how little their happiness and satisfaction with your company matters to you. And that's the wrong direction. Who wants to return to a company where they aren't valued or important?

HOMEWORK ASSIGNMENT:
OVERDELIVERING

Newbies:

Are you prepared to overdeliver?

What are some ways you can expand value and give more than your customers or clients anticipate?

Existing Business Owners:

Have you cut back on services to save on expenses?

What are some ways that you can bring service to the forefront and begin to overdeliever?

> How can you show your customers or clients how important and valued they are?

Handling Mistakes

Have you ever been a customer with a company that made a mistake? Most of us have. It's not uncommon. But the *worst* mistake a company can make is to handle mistakes poorly. In fact, a mistake is an opportunity to regain your clients' faith and trust in your company.

Obviously, it's better not to make mistakes in the first place, but if a mistake *is* made, there are ways to go above and beyond the call of duty to repair the damage *and* the customer relationship.

Admit It

The first step in handling a mistake is to admit it. You don't have to throw a team member (or yourself) under the bus to accomplish this goal, but you do have to admit to the customer that a mistake was made and you're going to take responsibility for fixing it.

Apologize for It

Let your customer know you're sorry the mistake happened and you're sorry he or she was inconvenienced by it. It's simple, really. When you apologize sincerely and express genuine regret that a mistake was made, people appreciate it.

Solve It

Whatever the problem is, solve it. Empower your employees to solve mistakes too, so your clients don't have to wait for things to get resolved. Fix whatever's broken. Replace whatever isn't working. Whatever it takes, make it right.

Repair the Damage

Repairing the damage may not be easy. The admission, the apology, the resolution, they go a long way, but sometimes they're not enough. Be prepared to offer a refund, a discount on a future purchase, or just something nice. Empower your employees to do the same so clients never have to wait.

HOMEWORK ASSIGNMENT:
HANDLING MISTAKES

Newbies:

What kinds of mistakes do you anticipate you (or your staff) might make in your business?

How can you handle these mistakes in an extraordinary way that repairs the damage and makes your customers delighted with you?

Existing Business Owners:

How are mistakes currently handled in your business?

What are some ways that you can improve the way mistakes are handled?

Can you empower your employees so that they can fix mistakes and repair the damage?

THE VILLAGE

THE VILLAGE

No man is an island, entire of itself; every man is a piece of the continent, a part of the main...

—JOHN DONNE,
Devotions Upon Emergent Occasions (1624)

The road of an entrepreneur can be lonely. It can feel as if you're in this by yourself and there's no one to help you, like you're out there on your own.

They say "It takes a village to raise a child," but it also takes a village to grow a business. As you forge ahead into entrepreneurship, you need to create a village of your own.

Some may call it a tribe, some call it a community, but I love the idea of a village. When I think about my business and the people I've surrounded myself with—colleagues, clients, peers, friends, and the people from whom I buy products and services—I see a tight-knit community of people who are all joined by a similar aim: providing the best products and services and delivering the most extraordinary experience to our clients and customers.

To avoid feeling like the solitary entrepreneur, you need a village. And to survive and grow, your business needs a village, too.

WHO YOU NEED IN YOUR VILLAGE

Every village needs four groups of people: masterminds, networks, administrators, and advisors. I'm going to show you what each group is for and how it can help you succeed faster.

Masterminds

Mastermind groups were first introduced in Napoleon Hill's book *Think and Grow Rich* (which should be a staple in every entrepreneur's library, one that's dog-eared and covered in notes, in my opinion). Hill first defined the concept of a mastermind as, "coordination of knowledge and effort, in a spirit of harmony, between two or more people, for the attainment of a definite purpose."

> **" "It takes a village to raise a child," but it also takes a village to grow a business. "**

A mastermind is a group designed to achieve a specific outcome by the coordination of the knowledge and effort of its members. That's cool, right? I mean, think about it: You and a few other people join forces to, say, support each other's goals, market each other's businesses, and give each other advice and feedback. How amazing is that?

Hill talked about the economic advantages that stem from mastermind groups. The "advice, counsel, and personal cooperation of a group of men who are willing to lend him wholehearted aid, in a spirit of perfect harmony" can actually lead to all of the members of the group prospering financially.

If you've formed a group of like-minded entrepreneurs who are cooperating in a spirit of "perfect harmony," willing to lend one another "wholehearted aid" and give each other advice, feedback, support, and encouragement, aren't you going to feel positively toward the others in the group? And aren't you going to be more likely to refer business to them, not because you've been forced to do so by the rules of the group, as so many networking groups require, but because you respect your fellow mastermind members and want to see them excel and flourish?

There's more to masterminding than financial prosperity. In *Think and Grow Rich*, Hill also said, "No two minds ever come together without, thereby, creating a third, invisible, intangible force which may be likened to a third mind." This is really a "the whole is more than the sum of its parts" idea, where, when you bring multiple minds together, you can create far more than each of you can create individually, simply because of the brilliant chemistry that comes from the fusion of two people spinning ideas back and forth, riffing on each other's ideas, expanding them, and suggesting new things.

How Masterminds Work

Every mastermind group is different, but true mastermind groups that work best are ones that have regularly scheduled meetings for the full group and give each member a time to bring issues to the group for discussion, feedback, help, and idea generation. While there might be a founder of the group, there is no leader. Instead, each member takes responsibility for keeping the group going and participating in meetings.

Thanks to modern technology, you don't have to be located in the same geographical location as your mastermind members. You can use video chats to connect and still accomplish the same goals. However, when you're meeting virtually, it's useful to schedule an annual year-end mastermind retreat where members can meet in the same place and connect for a couple of days to hammer out plans for the next year.

Masterminds seem to work best when they're limited to a maximum of eight or ten people. Any more than that and you'll have chaos, and there'll never be enough time for each member during meetings.

Some mastermind groups build in "accountability partners" so that pairs of members get together in between mastermind meetings to hold each other accountable to stated goals and plans. This isn't necessary, but it is a nice bonus if it works for your group.

Your mastermind can be as formal or informal as you want. You can set up a private, password-protected web site to serve your group or not. You can have a strict set of rules or loose guidelines. Allow the personality of the group to determine how much formality is required.

How to Create a Mastermind

Though there's an enormous amount of flexibility in a mastermind and how it's constructed, masterminds must possess certain characteristics in order to be successful. Each characteristic is necessary for the mastermind to work for all the members.

Chemistry

Like when you hire employees and make sure they're a good fit for the corporate culture, similarly, make sure each member is a good fit with the chemistry of the group.

You don't need members to be identical in their thinking and working styles, In fact, it's better if they're not. You'll get better and more creative ideas from one another if you're all a little different. You're looking for good chemistry, so members of the group do need to get along.

Commitment

Choose members who are committed to and have time for the group so that the group is an important part of their business success, not an after-thought. Without a strong commitment to the group from every member, things will fall apart quickly.

Require a yearlong commitment from each member. At the end of the year, you can decide if the group has been useful and recommit. Members should plan to stay in the group for the full year. Try to avoid adding new members mid-year, as you don't want to disrupt the flow of your group. Reserve new membership nominations for the year end when you may have members who decide to leave.

Purpose

Mastermind groups succeed when they're formed around a shared vision, a common goal, or a single purpose. Andrew Carnegie's mastermind group was formed around the promotion of the steel industry. A few friends of mine are in a mastermind formed around the common goal of creating content for their businesses. My husband is in a mastermind group with other business owners in the music industry to help each other grow by sharing resources, experiences, and distribution opportunities. Other masterminds are focused on a shared vision of creating a specific kind of change in the world.

There is no "right" answer here. You can create whatever kind of mastermind you want, but you need a purpose to guide your group. Every member should be clear on what that purpose is from the start.

Regularity/Consistency

More mastermind groups have failed due to a lack of regularity and consistency than any other factor. If you don't meet regularly and consistently, you won't be able to pursue the purpose of your group.

Groups should meet at least once every other week, but at the minimum, you should meet once a month and at the maximum, once a week. If you meet less than once a month, your members will experience a much looser level of interest and commitment, while if you meet more than once a week, you'll easily overtax your members and take up too much time. A mastermind group shouldn't take up so much time that it interferes with the work that members need to do to run a business.

Trust

Members of any mastermind group must be able to trust one another. Everything that happens within the confines of a mastermind group should be considered absolutely confidential at the highest levels so that members can share freely without any concern for their privacy or intellectual property.

You can have a confidentiality or non-disclosure agreement for your mastermind or choose members extremely wisely and carefully and have a "gentleman's agreement." Either way, trust in a mastermind group is imperative to its success.

HOMEWORK ASSIGNMENT:
MASTERMINDS

Newbies:

Make a list of people who are starting businesses or who are in your industry whom you could work with to create a mastermind. Consider inviting some people who are already successful in business as well.

Write an e-mail to each person, inviting him or her to participate in a mastermind with you. Outline what your goal for the group is, what the group will be like, what guidelines you'd like to impose, how often you'd like to meet, and how you'd like it to work overall.

Send out a few invitations and wait to hear back before sending out more. Try to keep your group to eight to ten members.

Existing Business Owners:

Make a list of goals that you would like to get out of creating a mastermind group.

Choosing one or two of the goals from your list, list some other business owners who might also be interested in pursuing those goals.

Write an e-mail to each person, inviting him or her to participate in a mastermind with you. Outline what your goal for the group is, what group will be like, what guidelines you'd like to impose, how often you'd like to meet, and how you'd like it to work overall.

Send out a few invitations and wait to hear back before sending out more. Try to keep your group to eight to ten members.

Networks

For many people, networking isn't fun. There's nothing more painful than dressing up in uncomfortable clothes, packing a pocket full of business cards, and heading to a meeting where everyone there is trying to get someone else to hire them in some capacity.

Let's face it, most networking events are an endless stream of recruitment speeches, pitches and self-promotion, and business cards being shoved into your hand. You experience all manner of handshakes: Sweaty Hand, Clammy Hand, Overly-Firm Shake, Wispy Shake, Dead Hand, Fish Hand, and last, Delicate Lady Shake, all of them awful. And don't even get me started on the futility of the "speed networking" event.

> **" Too many people walk into a networking environment with the mindset of getting business rather than giving value. "**

The challenge here is that people are *trying to network*. We do business with people, but too many people focus on the business and not the people in the business. Plus, far too many people walk into a networking environment with the mindset of *getting* business rather than *giving* value.

Networking works, but for long-term success focus on the human beings you interact with and what value you can bring to the table for them.

Do better than learning what people do for a living—*get to know them* so that you can get a feel for what they're like to work with. Business relationships are Matchmaking 101: Everybody doesn't click with the same people you click with. So it's okay if you already have an accountant or a realtor or an event planner of your own. If, in your networking, you've gotten to know the person more than the business, whether your best friend or the woman you just met at yoga class asks you if you know a great event planner, you know the perfect person to send them to, because that event planner you met last week will meet their needs, *and* they'll like each other.

> **" Networking works, but for long-term success focus on the human beings you interact with and what value you can bring to the table for them. "**

Plus, everyone has different needs. The person I would choose to handle my complex, eighty-year-old pipes might not be the same person you might need to handle the plumbing on your brand-new house. Maybe one graphic designer is great at creating those sweet, feminine designs you see used for bakeries and baby boutiques. Maybe another one is great at cutting-edge, technological-looking designs.

The challenge is that networking groups rarely work the way they should. They're often insulated groups that only allow one of each kind of businessperson to join. So you're stuck with whatever you get. What happens if you don't think someone in the group is very good at what they do? What if you just don't *like* someone in the group or if you think they're a little shady? Are you still supposed to send business to them?

So how do you build an amazing network for your village if what exists in networking groups isn't working?

How to Build a Great Network

The best way to build a great network is to dive in and get to know a lot of people. Weed out the people who aren't nice or who aren't good at what they do, and what you're left with is a group of great people who are really good at what they do. That way you can recommend the right person for the right job when the time comes.

How you accomplish that goal should be guided by your personality and how much time you have available. If you love going out and meeting people and that's your "thing," then get out there in the real world. If you're not necessarily a "people person" and prefer to network via social media, that's OK, too.

No matter where or how you're networking, though, you need to build a few things into your mindset and vocabulary to make it work:

Value

Before you go into any networking space or conversation, take a moment to get into the "value mindset." Prepare yourself to focus your attention on the other person in every conversation. Listen to what he or she has to say. While they're talking, don't worry about how you can help or even respond—in fact, try to quiet your "brain talk" so that you can really listen to other person. When he or she has finished, *then* think about what value the other person needs and how you can contribute.

> **When you're networking, don't worry about making your pitch. Don't look for an angle or an opportunity when you can start talking about your business. Just focus on the other person.**

This mindset is the opposite of finding ways to contribute so you can get hired. It's not about how you can offer them your services or lead the discussion into a sales conversation. It's about bringing value to other people and making a positive difference to them. Maybe this conversation turns into a business relationship later or maybe it doesn't, but what's most important in that moment is that you bring *value.* (For more on this idea, read *The Go-Giver*, by Bob Burg and John David Mann. It's a great book that should be in every small business owner's library.)

Don't worry about making your pitch. Don't look for an angle or an opportunity when you can start talking about your business. Just focus on the other person.

If this is the first time you've heard advice like this, you may think it's counterintuitive to growing your business. If that's you, I challenge you: Try it for ninety days. See how it feels, and watch where your business goes.

Curiosity

When you're in a networking space or conversation, get curious about the people around you. Ask about things that aren't related to business and try to get to know them as human beings. There's more to networking than just "tell me what you do."

You don't do business only with what people *do*. You do business with who people *are*. Get curious about people and networking gets more interesting *and* productive. You might find people who you want become friends with *and* who you get to do business with. What's better than that?

Memory

There are two ways memory is important in networking. First, *your* memory is important. Once you meet someone, you should remember that person's name. There are many strategies for remembering names, but the one that I've found most effective is to look every new person in the eye, study their face (and smile, otherwise it's creepy), and use their name right away, as in, "It's nice to meet you, John." Then, imagine that you have a Sharpie marker and visualize writing their name across their foreheads. See the name there for a few moments and let it fade. This should help you to remember his or her name.

Second, being *memorable* also matters. You want people to remember you in a positive light. Spend the entire time you're with other people talking about yourself or your business, and people will remember you as "that guy who talked about himself the entire time," and not, "that nice guy who runs that restaurant down the street." When you become memorable as a pleasant, interested-in-other-people person, people *want* to patronize your business, even without you having to sell it to them. Remember, people do business with people they *like*.

Staying In Touch

You're likely to walk away from networking events and conversations with business cards from the people you've talked to. As soon as a conversation ends, take notes on each business card with hints to remind you about the conversation that you had. That way you'll associate the card with the person.

As soon as you get home, sit down and write a note to the people you just met. Not an e-mail, but a handwritten note. Let them know it was nice to have met them, you'll be glad to send business their way whenever you can, and you look forward to talking with them again. Put your cards in the mail immediately.

Handwritten notes are uncommon in this day and age. E-mails are so much simpler; we often forget how wonderful a tangible piece of mail is… until we receive one. Sending a handwritten card makes you memorable and distinct. People sit up and take notice of someone who does that. Don't shortcut the note.

Add your new acquaintances to your holiday mailing list and connect with them on social media platforms. *Never* add them to your e-mail list without their permission!

HOMEWORK ASSIGNMENT:
NETWORKING

Newbies and Existing Business Owners:

- Read *The Go-Giver*, by Bob Burg and John David Mann.
- Connect with people rather than with businesses.
- Focus on the other person, and experiment with listening and bringing value.
- Send a handwritten note to each person you meet.

Administrative

Another group you need in your "business village" is the administrative group. This group is made up of people who provide goods and services that help your business run better. These are people like your web developer, graphic designer, sales team, assistants, and other staff members.

Creating a strong, efficient, competent administrative group in your village means getting certain ducks in a row.

Needs

Before you hire anyone, assess your needs now and in the future. A great resource for this process is Michael Gerber's *The E-Myth: Why Most Businesses Don't Work and What To Do About It.*

Create three organizational charts (I draw mine like flowcharts). The first flowchart is your business as it stands now. The second is where you want your business to be at its peak. The third is an intermediate step, where you'll be in, say, a year or two. Identify all the people you want working in and for your business and how you want the hierarchy structured (see the book web site for examples: http://BusinessInBlueJeans.com/book).

Once you've created your charts, identify responsibilities for each position in the chart. Then, map out each task for every job and keep all the tasks for one job in its own binder (or if you're like me, in an online, editable document). This specificity allows you to get clear on what kind of person you want in each position *and* makes training a lot easier.

Hiring

In the last chapter, I talked about hiring in the context of creating a workforce that's highly qualified *and* fits into the culture of your organization. This kind of hiring (and the accompanying compensation structures I mentioned) produces happier, satisfied, engaged employees that actually *want* to do their jobs and will do them well.

As you look toward expanding your business and hiring new staff members, hire with a specific corporate culture in mind. Outline that corporate culture and get a sense of what you want your company to be like for your employees and for yourself, so that you can tell early on whether someone's going to fit into the mix.

Be sure to find out the federal and state laws governing what you can and can't ask someone in an interview. For the most part, you can't ask about anything involving race, gender, religion, marital status, age, disabilities, ethnic background, country of origin, health, or sexual preference, but the state laws may vary, so find out what the rules are for your state.

Training

One of the most important parts of creating a strong administrative group is training them well, not just in the specifics of their jobs, but also in the company culture.

Even if you've created a handbook for each position in your organizational chart, you still need to train each employee. When someone joins your organization, it can be daunting to follow a step-by-step manual for every task. Many people also learn better by watching others. Provide a variety of ways for new hires to learn and create a structure for including them and welcoming them into the corporate culture.

Finally, if you can, create a training budget for each employee so that she or he can stay current on and expand his or her skills, becoming an even more substantial asset to your team.

Alternatives

Today, with the available technology, you don't have to hire staff immediately. In fact, you can hire a contractor who can do much of the same work at a fraction of the cost, so you don't have to take the leap to bring on a full-time staff member and pay salary plus benefits and more.

Of *course* it's great to be a "job creator," but if you try to grow your business too quickly, hiring staff that you may not need, may not have time to train, and may not be prepared to pay for (considering salaries and benefits), you may find yourself in trouble and with far more overhead than you expected.

Outsourcing

Small business owners often say, "I can't outsource. I don't know what I would have someone else do. I don't know how to tell them how to do it. I don't even know how to find someone to do this stuff." But some start out with, "I don't know *why* I would outsource anything."

Before I get too far into this, let me say that "outsource" does not mean "sending jobs overseas." Indeed, you can save some money by hiring freelancers in Asia and the Middle East, but that does not mean that you have to or that you should.

There are certainly pros and cons for outsourcing to other countries, but the biggest issue I have found with working with professionals who speak

English as a second language is that you often spend an inordinate amount of time dealing with a language barrier. Even if your freelancer is fluent, language has subtle nuances, and these subtleties are critically important when you're dealing with, say, a logo for your brand, and you want to make sure that the logo strikes *precisely* the right tone for your business. At the least, if you decide to hire contractors who are from a different country than you, make sure you speak to them and can ascertain their language fluency and understanding of nuance. This will save you a *lot* of time and trouble down the road.

Why Outsource?

Several authors have carefully detailed the benefits and reasons for outsourcing, most notably Timothy Ferriss, author of *The 4-Hour Work Week*, so I won't belabor it here. The most important things you need to know about why outsourcing is smart are:

1. There are tasks in your business that require skills or knowledge you don't have.

2. There are tasks in your business that you aren't good at.

3. There are tasks in your business that you don't like.

4. There are tasks in your business that you can have someone else do while you use your time on revenue-generating activities.

I talk to business owners all the time who tell me things like, "I spent an ungodly amount of time trying to learn how to make a web site, but I finally gave up and hired someone else." In most cases, small business owners try to do things themselves first to save money. But are you *really* saving money if you spend countless hours learning how to do something, instead of hiring a qualified professional who can do the same work better and in far less time than it would take you to get up to speed in the first place? The answer is no.

Let's say you decide to design your own logo. You try a few different freeware software downloads to experiment, learn how to use the software, try out different fonts, color schemes, ask your Ten for feedback...by the time you're done, maybe you've spent forty hours on this project. If you charge $100 per hour, you've lost the $4,000 you could've earned while you spent time on this project. Plus, you may not have a very good logo.

Now let's say you decide to hire someone to design a logo for you. You research logo design firms, hire one, give them all the information they need, and go back and forth with concepts until you choose a logo. Maybe this takes you ten hours and the logo costs $1,000. You're still up $2,000.

Even better, if you get a referral for a graphic designer from someone you trust (you'll find some of my favorites on the book web site: http://BusinessInBlueJeans.com/book), then you'll cut that time down to maybe five hours and the logo cost down to $500. Now you've saved $3,000 over doing it yourself. See how this works?

Outsourcing done right can save you a *ton* of time, energy, money, and yes, even angst. And the math gets even simpler. You can do your own market research, spending your own time at a value of $75/hour, when you could be working with clients and earning that money, or you can hire a contractor to do the research for you at $15/hour instead.

> ❝ **Outsourcing done right can save you a ton of time, energy, money, and yes, even angst.** ❞

Remember, just because you've freed up some of your own time doesn't mean you can slack off. If you don't use that time to generate income, you're not losing $75/hour, you're losing $90/hour because you're not earning income *plus* you're paying someone that $15/hour. If you book clients for the time when you're paying your freelancer, you're still netting $60/hour (not including other expenses, obviously).

See how that works?

When Outsourcing Goes Horribly Wrong

Let's look at another scenario, a story I've heard over and over from small business owners:

Let's say you decide to create your own web site. This is common for entrepreneurs who are just starting out. Web sites are a big expense, and you want to save where you can. You don't know how to make a web site, so you try the automated, "Easy To Use! One-Click and Have Your Very Own Web Site!" that your domain registrar offers. You quickly realize that your new "easy" web site is ugly, looks homemade, and is a dismal failure.

You decide to hire a guy from church who says he does web sites. You pay him a couple hundred bucks and tell him what you want your web site to look like. He creates a web site that looks, unsurprisingly, like a church web site, which is not at all what you hoped for. It takes him three weeks.

Finally you decide to hire a freelancer, and you go to a well-known freelance web site and post a job listing. You get forty or fifty applications to your job, but the only ones that are within your budget are from Third World countries, and most of those clearly didn't understand your job listing, have no portfolio or a poor portfolio, or they have no feedback from other jobs.

You choose one of the few remaining candidates and start the project. At first, you're in regular communication with your contractor, but then things start to slow down. You don't hear from your web designer for a couple of days, then a week, then…nothing. Your contractor disappears with your initial payment.

At this point, you're done with the freelancing web sites, and you head straight to your local web design firm in town and hire them on the spot. They quote you $8,000 (or more) for a simple web site, plus $250/year for annual hosting, but you are so frustrated by this point that you don't care. You take it. You'll take anything at this point.

The site you end up with is fine, and it looks very professional. But here's what you don't know:

1. The web site you just paid $8,000 for should have cost a quarter of that or less (as of the writing of this book).

2. Annual domain name renewal and web hosting shouldn't cost more than $60/year in most cases (as of the writing of this book).

3. Behind the scenes, your site may be working against you with search engines. What most web site owners don't know is that the code you never see has to be tidy and include important, useful information that search engines need to catalog and rank your site. If you don't know how to look at that code, you may not even show up in Google or any other search engine.

This is how outsourcing goes wrong. This is how outsourcing gets a bad rap. It breaks my heart and makes me mad every time I hear stories like this. Believe me, I've heard a ton of them. In fact, that's one of the reasons I started assembling my own team of superheroes in the first place, so that I could protect my clients from these outsourcing villains.

Protecting Yourself

How can you protect yourself from this kind of time-wasting, money-sucking nightmare?

The truth is, there are no real guarantees. If you opt to work with an individual contractor, even if they're awesome, there's always the possibility that they might get sick or, God forbid, have a death in the family. One way you can protect yourself against this kind of problem is by hiring companies with built-in redundancies so that if your designer or programmer or copywriter or assistant quits or gets sick, there's someone in place to fill in.

If you're using one of the popular freelancing sites, some of them have a lot of structure built into their sites to provide protection for the buyers. Their systems are set up so that you can opt to pay into escrow accounts, pay only when milestones are reached, and even, in some cases, check screenshots of your workers' computers to make sure they're really doing what they say they're doing.

However, contractors have developed workarounds so that they can fool the system. On one popular site, for example, workers regularly delete certain screenshots that show personal activity. Or, if you choose to hire an overseas team, you'll find that your workers may converse via on-screen chat in a language you don't know, so you don't know if they're talking about your project, something personal, or worse, someone else's project. On the whole, you really won't be able to do a lot to protect yourself from things like this.

You can check reviews and feedback on freelance web sites, but they may not always tell the whole story. If you are going by feedback, choose contractors with a *lot* of feedback, as in double digits, preferably even hundreds. Read the comments, especially, I'm sorry to say, the negative ones.

When you find negative feedback, the way the review is written can give you a good clue about whether the problem was the client or the provider and whether the negative feedback is really justified. If the provider can provide a comment on the feedback, you'll get a good idea about how that person handles unsatisfied clients.

Even if you check a freelancer's reviews carefully and make a wise choice based on that feedback, you still may end up hiring someone who doesn't do very good work, plain and simple.

When you hire a freelancer, try to make your payments based on milestones. For example with a web site, you might pay half upfront, then half upon completion of your site, or you might be able to pay at smaller milestones along the way so you can more carefully track your freelancer.

Stay in contact with your contractor. Don't pester him or her with daily e-mails, but be clear that you expect to hear from him or her at least once a week, depending on the project, with updates. Keep the lines of communication open.

So How Do You Choose A Freelancer?

The real challenge to outsourcing is finding high-caliber, reliable people who will perform your tasks at a price you can afford. There are several ways to find reliable help, and most come with pros and cons.

The more popular web sites where freelancers lurk around looking for jobs can be good resources, but as you've seen in previous sections, you can't always trust that these systems will protect you. You can get references from your peers or ask someone you respect for their recommendations on professionals, but again, there are no guarantees.

If you don't have a coach, consultant, or mentor guiding you, then the best way to find amazing, talented freelancers is to become your own best detective. Learn to ask the right questions to get to the bottom of whether someone will be a good provider of services for your company. Use the same techniques I taught you for researching your peers to research any freelancer you're considering.

Before you start searching, come up with a list of your non-negotiables for whom you will and won't work with. As a guide, here are mine:

1. **Service providers must have a commitment to delivering** *legendary* **work product**. Anyone who does business with me knows that I'm a tough cookie, and I don't stop until my clients are delighted, yes, *delighted*, with their results.

That's why I need people who are exceptional at what they do and willing to go to the ends of the earth to make sure they've thrilled their clients.

2. **Service providers must be pleasant to work with and leave their ego at home.** I love working with people who are friendly, pleasant, and happy to accommodate a client's requests, who never complain, and who have no ego involved in the work. The last thing you want is to work with someone who acts as if they're doing you a huge favor by deigning to work with you. That's gross. It's important that my team cares about my clients and their dreams so that they can be active and involved in helping our clients make their dreams a reality. That's what we do. So if a freelancer or professional is more concerned about their ego than about my client's dream, they're not likely to make it past the first few minutes of working with me. In addition to caring about my clients, people who join my team also have to care about the other folks on our team and work well with them. No one on my team ever, ever throws anyone else "under the bus." It's a supportive, collaborative work environment where everyone shares the same goal: to make our clients' business dreams come true.

3. **Service providers must go above and beyond and deliver more than the client is paying for.** I work only with providers who do extraordinary work that my clients and I feel good about so that all of my clients walk away feeling that they got an incredible value and are likely to refer others to us. Many people deliver only what they think they can get away with—the bare minimum. I believe in exceeding clients' expectations so much that they're absolutely blown away.

These are *my* requirements, my non-negotiables. Yours might be different. But it's important that you have some set parameters so that you know when you have someone who fits the bill.

A NOTE ON TIMELINE AND BUDGET

You may be wondering why timeline and budget don't feature in my list of non-negotiables. If you're committed to delivering extraordinary, legendary work for your clients, then you are already taking their budget and timeline into consideration.

There's more that you need to know about this subject, however.

The old adage, "You get what you pay for," is both true *and* false when it comes to service providers. In fact, I think there's a Bell curve relationship here. Look at the chart below:

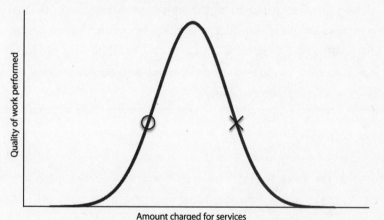

Amount charged for services

See the "O" on the left side and the "X" on the right side? There's a point where, if you're being charged way too little (anything to the left of the "O") or way too much (anything to the right of the "X") for services, chances are, something's wrong. This isn't a hard and fast rule, but rather something I've learned along the way.

On every project, conduct some research to get an overall sense of how much things should cost. Sometimes you'll discover a pretty big range. Some things (like web sites) are based on the complexity of the project. Other things are based on the complexity of the service you'll receive.

For example, if you've done your own market research and know your target market inside out, you should have a pretty good idea of what they'd respond to. Plus, you have The Ten to refer to as your small focus group. When you get your logo done, you should be able to get it done fairly inexpensively. However, if you search logo pricing, you'll discover that there are some freelancers that charge almost nothing to design a logo, while there are graphic design or marketing firms that charge exorbitant rates to develop the entire visual styling of a brand. On the low end, your freelancer might be using stock art to create a generic-looking logo. On the high end, your design firm may conduct a certain amount of focus group testing. Since you have your focus group already, you don't need that level of service.

Select the best provider for the specific task or project that you're working on. Get quotes from multiple providers and then ask questions. Research each provider and check his or her history as best you can. Don't automatically go for the lowest bidder out of fear or lack of resources, and don't go for the highest bidder because you're too tired to conduct more research.

How to Outsource

The first, best step to outsourcing is to make a list of the tasks that you really don't like doing and the tasks that you really aren't good at doing. My list includes things like accounting, graphic design, certain kinds of research, and setting up "backstage" technology.

I'm not good at graphic design—okay, I'm *terrible* at graphic design—and I find most of those other tasks to be really, really boring activities. A lot of people love doing these things, so why not let them do them for me?

Outsourcing can take two forms:

1. *Temporary outsourcing*—when you hire someone to perform a task that only needs to be done once. Examples of temporary outsourcing are designing a web site, conducting market research, or editing your book.

2. *Ongoing outsourcing*—when you have an ongoing task that needs to be performed continuously or repeatedly. Examples of ongoing outsourcing include phone answering, customer service, sales, accounting, and bookkeeping.

Once you've made your list of items to outsource, categorize each item into temporary and ongoing lists. When you start interviewing, you'll be able to give a very clear picture of what you're looking for to your candidates.

If you can, create as many step-by-step instructions as possible, especially for the ongoing tasks on your list. You should already be doing this for the future expansion of your business. Once you outline the steps in each task, it's easy to outsource that task with minimal training required.

You may not be able to create your step-by-step instructions because the tasks haven't been performed yet. It's okay if you need help, especially if they're things you're not very good at or don't know how to do. In fact, you might make creating a description of the steps needed to do the task part of your professional's job.

You may not hire the same person to handle all of your outsourced activities. You'll find generalists who can handle a variety of tasks, but you may not want to turn something that requires specialized knowledge like, say, accounting, over to them. I've had one assistant who handled a great many tasks herself, and a team of assistants handling a variety of different tasks based on their skills and competencies.

Decide whether you want to manage a team of people. You may not have the time to manage an entire team. Or you may not have had experience leading a team and may not want to manage your own projects. You can hire a project manager or an online business manager to handle your team for you.

The more layers between you and the people doing the work, the more you'll have to work to stay in touch with the ground floor. Even when you're outsourcing tasks, you should stay in touch with those who represent your company and/or perform tasks for you.

HOMEWORK ASSIGNMENT:
YOUR ADMINISTRATIVE TEAM

Newbies:

As you start your business, what kinds of tasks do you want or need to hire someone else to do?

> Which of those tasks can you outsource to a freelancer or virtual assistant?
>
> How much can you budget for these tasks?
>
> For each position or task that you've decided to outsource or hire for, list the responsibilities and map out each one, step by step.
>
> ### Existing Business Owners:
>
> If you have employees, have them list out their job responsibilities and map out each responsibility with step-by-step instructions. Their job has just expanded to include maintaining these instructions.

Advisory

There is one more group that you need in your village, and it's perhaps the most important group of all (but then, I may be a little biased). Your advisory group is paramount to your success. Included in your advisory group are your legal team, accounting team, and mentoring team.

> ## A NOTE ON BUSINESS STARTUPS
>
> Starting a business, from the standpoint of paperwork, is fairly simple. In many states, you can file your setup paperwork online for a small fee, and then you can head on over to the IRS web site to file to get your tax ID number.
>
> That said, it makes good sense to consult with a lawyer and an accountant before starting your business. First, you have to choose the type of business you're starting, which means you have to decide if you're going to be a sole proprietorship, a partnership, a limited liability company, or a corporation. The format you select depends on the legal and financial protections you need as well as your intentions for the company down the road.
>
> It's also worth your time to consult with an attorney to have him or her draw up your operating agreement, which can be written to build in specific protections so, for example, you avoid losing control of the company in certain circumstances. There are web

sites where you can have an inexpensive operating agreement made up for you, and it's fine for the short term, until you're making a small profit with your business and can have something better made up (visit the book web site at http://BusinessInBlueJeans.com/book for some resources).

However, if you're in a partnership, you should each meet with your attorneys and negotiate a sound operating agreement that has conditions you can both agree to. This will protect you and could even save your friendship down the road. I've seen several friendships destroyed over business, simply because they didn't have a properly written agreement in place.

Legal Team

Your legal team is there to help you protect yourself and your ideas and stay out of trouble now *and* down the road. You'll definitely want a business attorney who can write up and review contracts. Have someone you can trust on your team, so that when a question comes up, you don't waste time searching for the right person. You'll already have him or her on speed dial.

Accounting Team

An accountant is one of your best assets in business. Your accountant will help you avoid costly mistakes, stay within the tax guidelines when it comes to hiring employees, and can even save you money. This is another person you want on speed dial.

Mentoring Team

My mentoring team is complex. I have an official mentor, a business coach, and a marketing consultant rolled into one. This is the only person I pay on a monthly basis to help me with my business. I can e-mail him with any questions, and we meet regularly to discuss marketing campaigns and the direction of my business. This is by far the most important and valuable relationship in my advisory team, because he keeps me accountable and moving forward.

I have other mentors, however. I've mentioned several of them in this book. Over the years, I've forged relationships with authors whose books I loved and successful entrepreneurs who have done extraordinary things. For example, I consider Bob Burg, Larry Winget, and David Meerman Scott to be among my "informal mentors." I've developed relationships with each of them so that, on rare occasions, I can send them an e-mail to ask a question about their specific areas of expertise.

I've called myself a business and marketing consultant for years, but when I work with my one-on-one clients, I am coach, consultant, strategist, marketer, brander, translator of technical language, and sometimes even friend, all rolled into one. Luckily, my history and experience allow me to occupy these multiple roles, but everyone doesn't fit into all categories.

When it comes to choosing your mentor, there are several ways in which you must find a good fit.

Training

People often wonder what kind of training a mentor, coach, strategist, or consultant should have. The truth is, it depends on what you want them to do for you. Unlike, say, the title "psychologist," none of the titles, "coach," "mentor," "strategist," or "consultant" comes with any legal requirements. Sadly, that means that there are a *lot* of unqualified people out there who are coaching and mentoring others.

> **Beware of anyone who makes huge promises (especially those with big dollar signs attached) or tells you that your business will grow extremely quickly with their help.**

So what do you need to look for in a mentor, in terms of training? It depends on what you're looking for and what you want help with. At the least, you want someone who has been successful in the area you're looking for help with.

For example, as you start or grow your business, you may need help getting clarity and plotting the course. Look for a coach or consultant who is good at marketing and who has helped successful business owners and entrepreneurs to become even more successful.

It's not necessarily important that the person you choose has an MBA or is a "certified" coach. Sometimes even with those labels, people aren't very good at mentoring or helping entrepreneurs move forward. What's more important than degrees or certifications is that the person you're working with has been successful in doing the kind of work you're asking for.

Talk to the professionals you're considering bringing into your village. Beware of anyone who is unwilling to have a conversation with you before being hired. Coaches and consultants worth their salt should never take on clients unless they know what the clients want and have taken the time to have a conversation to ensure that it's a good fit for *both* parties. Also beware of anyone who makes huge promises (especially those with big dollar signs attached) or tells you that your business will grow extremely quickly with their help. "Get rich quick" or anything that *sounds* like "get rich quick" is usually code for just the opposite.

When you do talk to your professionals, ask about their methodology. How can they help you? I've heard some people say, "I talk to my clients, and their businesses grow." That is *not* a methodology. Look for specific, concrete ways in which they'll help you and guide you.

Ask for references. Anyone who's reluctant to give them is someone you can cross off your list pretty easily. Request phone numbers and e-mail addresses for references, and do your detective work to make sure the references are real people. Then, call each one and ask about his or her experience working with the professional you're considering.

Personality

Look for someone with whom you mesh well. You shouldn't work with someone who can't connect with you. Coaching and mentoring relationships require a great deal of rapport and trust, which aren't always easy to build. You should be able to tell from an initial session if you'll be able to build that relationship together.

Try to get a sense of how fast professionals work, how technical they are, how well they explain things, even how fast they speak. You want to know if these people will mesh well with you. You don't necessarily have to be best friends, but you do want to know if these people will support you when you need it *and* be willing to call you out when necessary—you're not paying for a "yes man."

Most importantly, pay attention to how the professional pays attention to *you*. You want someone who is fully engaged and excited to work with you. You want someone who wants your business to grow and be successful and knows how to guide you to make that happen.

Ethics

There are far too many coaches and consultants out there who are, frankly, untrustworthy, and who will take your money and provide little to no help with your business in return. Few things truly infuriate me—this is one of them. Ethics matter to your business and to the relationship you have with your mentor. Avoid people who have shown questionable ethics in business, because they'll only lead you down that same path.

Too Many Cooks

It is possible to become too enthusiastic about finding mentors to guide you. Earlier, I mentioned that I have one official mentor and several informal mentors. It might seem like I have "too many cooks in the kitchen," but in fact, you really only want one person guiding you, otherwise you'll get confused and become unsure about which path to follow. I follow my formal mentor's advice and only dip into the wealth of my informal mentors' wisdom on very rare, expertise-specific occasions.

> **Remember that, while you've hired someone to help you, you have a responsibility to make the relationship work, too.**

Building the Mentoring/Coaching Relationship

As you build the mentoring relationship, it may take time to build trust and rapport. Remember that, while you've hired someone, you have a responsibility to make the relationship work, too.

Give Feedback

Mentors, coaches, consultants…we work best when we get some feedback from clients. I once had a client who didn't tell me for *four weeks* that he didn't understand half of the technical terms I had used. Without that feedback from him, without him stopping me in the first week to say,

"Wait, can you explain that?" or "I don't know what that means," I thought he understood everything I had been saying. When he finally 'fessed up, we had to go back and review all the things he hadn't understood.

If you don't understand something, say so. If you don't know how to do something, speak up. This is part of building trust. Trust your mentor enough to tell him or her when you need *more*.

Do the Work

When your mentor asks you to do something (e.g., the homework assignments in this book), do the work. Just having a mentor isn't enough to create success. Your mentor can only do so much.

> **You must be more invested in your success than anyone else. Do the work.**

You must be more invested in your success than anyone else, and that means you have to take the guidance your mentor gives you and implement suggestions, perform tasks, and *do the work*. Don't expect success to just appear without any effort. It just doesn't work like that.

A FEW
MORE WORDS

A FEW MORE WORDS

I wanted to put so much more into this book. Unfortunately, limitations of time and space only allowed me to write so much. However, because I wanted to give you as much help as possible, I've put loads of additional, bonus content on the book web site, http://BusinessInBlueJeans. com/book.

Remember, you're not alone. Entrepreneurship *can* be a lonely road, but it doesn't have to be. In fact, that's why you create your village. I'd love to be a part of your village and hear about your business adventures.

I've read a lot of books and have had the fortune to become friends with many of the authors just because I was brave enough to send an e-mail and ask a question or make a comment on the book. I don't want you to have to feel brave to send me an e-mail, so I'm just going to invite you to do so. If you have a question about something you've read in this book, drop me a line at susan@businessinbluejeans.com or tweet me @suebmoe.

Now go out there and make amazing things happen!

Warmly,
Susan Baroncini-Moe

JOIN THE BUSINESS IN BLUE JEANS COMMUNITY

Join the Business in Blue Jeans Community today and access even more additional, bonus content including videos, bonus chapters, and training materials. Membership is *free*, and you'll have access to others starting and running their own businesses, plus extra training to help you create an amazing, profitable business. I'm even including bonus chapters that I couldn't fit into the book, including chapters and videos on:

- Funding Your Startup and Growth

- Sales

- Negotiation

- Specific Marketing Strategies

- And much, much more!

Visit http://BusinessInBlueJeans.com/book/offer today!

ACKNOWLEDGMENTS

Many people made this book possible.

To Leo Baroncini, my husband, thank you for teaching me how to keep my creative mind fresh and for encouraging me to take naps when I needed to. And thank you for not minding when I wrote on my iPad during Open Mike Nights. You make my life better. You make me want to *be* better, every single day. Also, you make my belly hurt with giggles, and that's the best gift I ever received.

To my family: Dad, Beth, Anne, Alex, Claire, and Miles, thank you for believing in me and encouraging me as I wrote this book, and for making me leave the writing process now and then to spend much-needed time with family along the way. Thank you, Dad, for teaching me to think outside the box, and thank you, Anne, for teaching me to read, without which, this book would not have been possible.

To my mom, who always told me I could do anything I put my mind to, who used far too much underlining and way too many exclamation points, whose e-mails I keep in a special folder where I can read your words of encouragement every day. I miss you so, so much. I wish you could see me now.

To John Michael Morgan, thank you for being there for me, every step of the way, for telling me to write the book I wanted to write, and for showing me how to do so many things better. Your support, your encouragement, and your feedback were invaluable.

To Bob Burg and John David Mann, your books continually remind me how I really see the world and who I want to be.

To Larry Winget, thank you for answering so many of my questions and for being such an amazing example of how to just be who you are.

To Nathan Martin, David Wildasin, and the entire team at Sound Wisdom, thank you for supporting my dream for this book and making it a reality.

To Barbara Richard, who saved me from repetition and loose prose, and who was an exceptional steward of my words. I am in your debt. You totally rock, my sister. Rosie would be so proud.

To Ben Cope, thank you for taking care of my technical world so brilliantly. You *are* a genius.

To Chris Reimer, thank you for reading through sections that I thought might be boring and telling me that they weren't. Your feedback was super helpful and made me feel better.

To Michael E. Gerber, thank you for *The E-Myth* and the lessons within and for teaching me that there are no solo entrepreneurs.

To Seth Godin, thank you for writing so succinctly about so many key marketing points. You have taught me much throughout the years. One day, I *know* you'll say yes.

To the late, great Chet Holmes, thank you for your kind welcome to social media and for your encouragement. I miss your generous spirit.

To David Meerman Scott, thank you for teaching me so much, through your books and our conversations about speaking and marketing. I hope I'm half as amazing a speaker as you are when I grow up.

To Carolyn See, who wrote *Making a Literary Life*, thank you for being the first person to tell me that I was going to have to market my own books, way back then, so it didn't come as a surprise now. Thanks for the heads up.

To the Internet and information marketers who charge a fortune and deliver nothing, the "cookie-cutter approach" business coaches who can't keep their promises, and the scam artists who promise "get rich quick" schemes, thank you for giving me such a beautifully clear place to take a stance and draw a line in the sand.

To my clients, who are my unwitting guinea pigs and who occasionally had to wait a little bit longer for e-mails when I was in a writing frenzy, thank you for your patience. I couldn't ask for a better group of people to work with. You make every day interesting.

And to you, dear reader, thank you for reading this book all the way to the end. I'm grateful to you, and I'm impressed! Now go make business happen!

ENDNOTES

1. "About Google," *Google,* accessed October 25, 2012, www.google .com/about/company.

2. "Customer Service Isn't Just a Department," *Zappos.com,* accessed October 25, 2012, http://about.zappos.com/.

3. "Our Mission Statement," *Virgin Atlantic,* accessed October 25, 2012, www.virgin-atlantic.com/en/us/allaboutus/missionstatement/index.jsp.

4. "About Southwest," *Southwest.com,* accessed October 25, 2012, www .southwest.com/html/about-southwest/index.html.

5. Joseph Berger, Bernard P. Cohen and Morris Zelditch, Jr. American Sociological Review, Vol. 37(3), June 1972, pp. 241-255. Murray Webster, Jr. and James E. Driskell, Jr. American Sociological Review, Vol. 89(1), July 1983, pp. 140-165.

6. Karen Dion, Ellen Berscheid and Elaine Walster. Journal of Personality and Social Psychology, Vol. 24(3), December 1972, pp. 285-290.

INDEX